21ST CENTURY SUPERVISION

By

Bert Nemcik, Ph.D.

The Lifelong Learning Network

Copyright © 2011

TABLE OF CONTENTS

PREFACE

...Of a good leader

who talks little

When his work is done,

his aim fulfilled,

They will say,

"We did this ourselves."

Lao-tzu

1. SUPERVISION DEFINED

The key to success for any organization whether it be a business, a government agency, a human services system, or and educational establishment is good supervision. In the past twenty years as a result of good supervision in America, the national output doubled (George, 1970). How has this minor miracle happened? Simply put, supervisors get things done through the efforts of other people. They accomplish the objectives of their organizations by directing the efforts of others. Whether the supervisory role is simple or complex, the goal is still the same: to get others to perform tasks up to their potential to maximize output and achieve results which support the mission of the organization.

Who are these supervisors? What do they do? What are their specific responsibilities? What kinds of qualities do the most effective supervisors possess? How do they use these qualities to "get others to perform tasks?" What are the present and future challenges facing supervisors as the world moves toward the 21st Century? It is the purpose of this paper to answer these questions.

There are three main levels of supervision. Top-level supervisors are the "big bosses" in charge of the whole operation. A CEO or the owner-manager of a small firm are examples of this level of supervision. Middle supervisors are above the first-line supervisors but are below the top-line supervisor. A principal in a school is a middle supervisor; he is below the Superintendent of a school system, but above the "head teacher" or chairperson of a department within a school. First-line supervisors are the key people in the managerial family that carry out the policies and directives of middle and top management through face-to-face contact with the workers. Within the Abraxas Foundation, my own organization, first-line supervisors are the individual treatment supervisors who manage staff members who in turn, provide treatment for the clients within the facility.

What daily tasks does a first-line supervisor face? Here are some of them:
- Talks to employees about job-related problems.

- Gives directions to employees.
- Dictates letters, memos, shift plans.
- Sets treatment direction.
- Interviews new employees.
- Reads mail, reports, etc.
- Attends supervisory meetings.
- Makes decisions regarding residents' treatment direction.
- Decides who will be promoted.

These are just a few of the many tasks which the first-line supervisor might confront on any given work day. He or she may also perform many nonsupervisory activities such as typing on the computer, studying a case file, doing case file reviews, or copying reports or other information for employees.

All these activities require two types of activities on the part of the supervisor: 1) Physical, or 2) Mental. Physical activities involve some form of communication, like telling someone face-to-face to do something or talking on the telephone to them, writing to them, or communicating by gestures. Mental activities cannot be seen by anyone. They are acts performed by the supervisor like thinking about a new project, a problem child, or developing goals and objectives for the treatment unit.

To be a successful supervisor at any level several competencies are necessary. These three key areas are:
1. Technical skills.
2. Human skills.
3. Conceptual skills.

In the treatment field, supervisors must possess the technical skills to role model the kinds of behaviors that the employees can see, hear, and feel, and then mirror themselves in their interventions with the clients they treat. The supervisor must understand the technical skills necessary to use a computer to assist the employees in producing progress reports, treatment plans, discharge summaries, and aftercare plans. He or she must also be able to write well enough to demonstrate how the employees should write these documents.

Human skills are those required to effectively work with people. These involve being aware of ones own feelings, beliefs, and attitudes about others. By maintaining a full measure of self-awareness, he or she can understand and accept the beliefs, and viewpoints that differ from his or her own. By recognizing these differences, a supervisor can do a better job of communicating his or her ideas to others. With human skills, a supervisor can be sensitive to the motivations and needs of others and can judge the probable effects various courses of action may have on employees. These skills need to be so much a part of the supervisor that he or she applies them continuously; they cannot be separated from him or her.

Supervisors need conceptual skills. These enable a person to visualize something in its entirety. A person with good conceptual skills can "see" and understand all parts of the business and how each part contributes to the whole organization. Again, using the treatment program in which I work, supervisors must be able to conceptualize the entire treatment milieu to which residents are exposed. He or she needs to understand the role of the counselors who provide direct care to the client, the life skills workers who oversee milieu management during the daytime and evening hours, and how these separate individuals all interact to provide the client with the fullest measure of treatment possible for the client.

With good conceptual and human skills, a supervisor will be able to visualize the effect that would result from giving a relatively new clinician a caseload he or she is not prepared to handle. The supervisor can see that it might cause him or her to feel inadequate in undertaking such a task. He or she will then provide guidance and support as the new counselor assumes responsibilities one step at a time thus ensuring that the new employee will not become initially overwhelmed.

An effective supervisor needs all three skills: **technical skills** so that he can understand and perform the technical activities required, **human skills** so that he can both motivate others and understand individual (and group) feelings and actions, and **conceptual skills** so that he can clearly understand and coordinate all the activities of the agency through wise decision making. Technical skills are in greatest need in the lower levels of an agency. Human skills, on the other hand, are in real need throughout every level of a firm. Conceptual skills are more critical at the higher levels (George, 1970).

Given this discussion, the question is what does a supervisor actually do to perform his or her work? How does he or she go about accomplishing the mission of the agency?

George (1959) listed several key steps the supervisor engages in while performing his responsibilities:

1. He must plan his work and establish objectives. This is called the **planning** function.
2. He must organize people and materials in order to coordinate activities and actions. This is the **organizing** function.
3. He must secure qualified personnel to do the work-- the **staffing** function.
4. He must direct the efforts of his employees--the **directing** function.
5. He must control the activities of his employees--the **controlling** function (p. 10).

Let's examine these functions to see what is necessary for the supervisor to effectively perform them.

Planning is a process of developing a course of action to accomplish something. It is a process of developing and formulating the course of action needed to accomplish agency objectives. Planning is not a function reserved for top and middle management alone. First-line supervisors are actively engaged every day in planning, although theirs is not as complex or extended into the future as the higher levels of management. A successful supervisor plans what needs to be done, who will do it, when it will be done, how it will be done, and so on. Without this planning by the supervisor, his or her treatment unit may well become disorganized, confused, and ineffective. Thoughtful and careful planning by a supervisor can do much to change him or her from a mediocre supervisor to an outstanding one ready for newer and greater challenges.

Organizing consists of:
1. Determining what activities need to be accomplished to get the job done.
2. Grouping and assigning these activities to employees.
3. Giving the employees the necessary authority to carry out the activities in a coordinated manner (George, 1970, p. 11).

All supervisors perform the function of organizing. Those at the top level are interested in the broader aspects of the firm, whereas, the first-line supervisor is primarily interested in organizing his or her own department so that the work can be accomplished in the most effective manner possible.

The staffing function covers all activities needed to recruit, hire, and retain individuals in the agency. In our system, Human Resources does this. However, the actual staffing patterns within a given treatment unit are overseen by the treatment supervisor. Staffing means putting people with skills and growth potential in spots where their skills are needed and they can grow.

Directing deals with influencing, guiding, or supervising subordinates in their jobs. It consists not only of telling them what to do, but most importantly, of explaining why the job needs to be done. It also involves a large amount of communication and, in most supervisory positions, consumes a greater part of a supervisor's workday.

The essence of controlling from a supervisory standpoint is simply that a supervisor must control people. If people are controlled properly, then actions and events will conform to plans. Essentially, control is the check-up part of managing. There are many theories of controlling employees.

Theory X and Theory Y management are just two which have received extensive review in all endeavors of management theory. McGregor (1960) contrasted two general modes of thought about how a manager should manage people. Theory X was his term for the traditional and still largely current philosophy of management. Theory Y was the emerging concept that promised to integrate the goals of the organization and its members.

Theory X holds that the so-called average person is inherently immature, that he or she is innately lazy, irresponsible, gullible, resistant to change, self-centered, and thus indifferent to organizational needs. The managerial practice in dealing with such persons is to apply external controls (harshly, or paternalistically or firmly but fairly). External control is clearly appropriate for dealing with truly immature individuals. While conceding that such behavior and attitudes are not manifestations of their inborn nature but the product of their experiences. Treat people as if they were children, he said--and thus chronically underestimate them, distrust them, refrain from delegating authority--and they will respond as children. Thus, in reacting to a myth (people are unchangeable and immature) with external controls, managers have stimulated subordinates' behavior, and this in turn perpetuated the myth and seemingly justified their practice, for the more one controls, the more one has to control and, as goes the old Chines expression, "He or she who rides a tiger can never dismount."

It was the success and failure of Henry Ford that led McGregor to propose the Theory Y management concept. Ford was successful in getting men to work for twice the going wage doing menial work that for a period of time proved satisfactory for those living below subsistence levels. But as the base of wealth broadened, these needs began to be fulfilled to the extent that the workers no longer were satisfied to work under such "purgatory" existence.

McGregor (1957) cited Maslow's (1954) hierarchy of needs to justify a need to change the focus for managers. He wrote:

> Management by direction and control fails under today's conditions to provide effective motivation of human effort toward organizational objectives. It fails because direction and control are useless methods of motivating people whose physiological and safety needs are predominant.

Thus a new management theory was necessary, one based on more valid premises about human nature and motivation. Whereas Theory X held that the average person was unalterably immature, Theory Y holds that humans are essentially or at least potentially mature.

Supporting this new theory, Kerzner (1982) wrote that the motivation, the potential for development, the capacity for assuming responsibility, the readiness to direct behavior toward organizational goals are present in people (p. 351).

Theory Y would lead to management practices that would work with rather than against the grain of human nature. The goal of management under Theory Y then, is to "arrange organizational conditions and methods of operations so that people can achieve their own goals best by directing their own efforts toward organizational objectives" (Kerzner, 1982, p. 355).

For a time, Theory Y was misconstrued by some as the soft version of Theory X. Theory Y permits access to the full range of management approaches from external to self-control. Where on the spectrum to peg one's approach depends on the supervisor's judgement of the subordinate's current state of development. For example, if the employee is new and inexperienced, rather close supervision and guidance may be necessary initially. But external control gradually decreases as the individual learns to make decisions and takes independent action (Haney, 1986).

A complete discussion of McGregor's work is not within the scope or purpose of this paper, but his premise is certainly one that continues to promote significant discussion in managerial circles in America and around the world.

The characters and qualities that make a successful supervisor are difficult to pinpoint precisely because some are more important than others. A Supervisor must be able to inspire his or her employees, motivate them, and direct their work. As described earlier, a supervisor must possess technical, human, and conceptual competence. Being open-minded is certainly essential. He or she must be able to search outside the everyday rut for a better method, a new policy, an improved way of doing things. A successful supervisor must be able to discover what a problem is in times of trouble. Many unsuccessful supervisors treat the symptom of the problem and not the problem. They may give aspirin for a headache (the symptom), when the real cause of the headache is eyestrain. The cure is to purchase glasses and not give aspirin.

George (1979) described The Successful Supervisor as possessing the following qualities. He or she should have/be:

1. ***Ambition - the desire to manage and grow.*** He should always be willing to learn, to develop new skills, to broaden his job. He should not be afraid to take a chance but instead should possess confidence that he will succeed.

2. ***A self-starter.*** He should think and move on his own initiative and not wait to be told by others to do something. To do this he needs self-confidence and courage to move ahead.

3. ***Able to think.*** This is perhaps the hardest task most people face. Most of us find it easy to do, to act, to perform. We have difficulty, however, in thinking clearly about a problem--our minds wander, we are distracted by noises or other problems, or we prefer to do things rather than think about how to solve problems.

4. ***Able to express himself clearly.*** The best idea in the world is worthless unless it is communicated well. Most supervisors spend most of their time communicating. Therefore, they need to do it well. We aren't talking about great speaking or great writing. What we are talking about instead is the basic ability that a supervisor needs to get ideas across clearly to his employees so that they can understand what he wants them to do.

5. ***A salesman, or possess the ability to "sell" an idea to his employees.*** Any idea that you think up and communicate to others needs to be "sold." Selling an idea--convincing others of its worth--is one of the supervisor's prime tasks. Selling a plan of action is a vital part of a supervisor's job of communicating to his employees.

6. ***Moral integrity.*** Truthfulness, honesty, and integrity should be so much a part of a supervisor that his subordinates will have total confidence in him and his actions.

7. ***Able to organize effectively.*** This is another very important attribute, because a supervisor is constantly called on to organize his own work as well as the work of his men in order to maximize output.

8. ***Willing to tackle hard problems and make tough decisions.*** Anyone can make an easy decision, but a good supervisor must be willing to tackle the hard problems and make tough or unpopular decisions.

9. ***The ability to work with and through other people.*** He has to be able to get along with others and to get them to do what needs to be done for the organization.

10. **_Dynamic and have the ability to inspire others._** This is that special something, which you can't put your finger on, that makes you want to follow the directions of and work with some leader.

11. **_The ability to size up others and recognize individual strengths_ and weaknesses.** This is a critical ability needed by supervisors in order to get the right man in the job, as well as to reject the unqualified applicant.

12. **_Likes people._** He should like to be with people and work with people. In fact, it is hard to visualize a supervisor who doesn't like his people, who doesn't have a sense of loyalty and feeling for his employees.

13. **_A balanced person._** This means that he should be levelheaded, understanding, firm, able to laugh, and fair.

14. **_The ability to delegate authority to others._** He should get satisfaction from seeing things done through the independent efforts of his employees.

15. **_A willingness to subordinate his own desires and wishes_ to those of the supervisors or bosses.** He will have to realize that he cannot have his own way over every matter but must instead submit to his bosses' wishes.

16. **_Level-headedness and wisdom._** He will need to mediate difficult situations and render fair and impartial answers to petitions.

17. **_A thorough understanding of what his job is and what he is supposed to do._** Knowing the technical aspects of his job will give him confidence and assurance in dealing with problems and in talking with employees.

18. **_Be able to win the friendship, loyalty, and support of his employees_ as well as of his other associates.** He will need to possess and show a spirit of willing cooperation with other supervisors in his division as well as in other areas of the firm.

19. ***A good mind and a good education.*** A good mind is reflected in an open and willing-to-learn attitude in tackling problems. A good education is not reflected in the number of years spent in school, but in the quality and amount of information he has absorbed. Experience in many instances can compensate for formal education.

20. ***To see the whole picture using conceptual skills*** **in order to understand what top and middle management want done and why.** To be a successful supervisor, he will need to understand the whole picture and communicate this in an understandable way to his fellow employees.

21. ***Patience.*** This is a virtue the supervisor will need to be successful. Patience to listen to and understand employees; patience to spend whatever time is needed to understand and improve work situations and worker relations; patience to take the time necessary to plan the total work flow and organize it in such a way that employees will feel comfortable in doing their jobs.

22. ***Flexible.*** Resisting change is one of the surest ways to slow down progress. Successful supervisors are the ones with open and receptive minds who do not resist change. They welcome new ideas, new ways to performing old jobs, and new concepts about how things can be improved.

23. ***Self-confident.*** A supervisor needs to have faith and confidence in his abilities and his capacity to plan, organize, and direct the efforts of others.

24. ***Initiative and the desire to succeed.*** If his desire to be a successful supervisor is strong enough, he may well overcome shortcomings that he sees in himself. Determination, willingness, and the strong desire to be a successful supervisor will put him well on the way to achieving his goal (pp. 14-16).

After reviewing these qualities, is it facetious to believe that one person can and must possess all of them to be successful? No, because no person can possess all of them at the same time immediately. These are a catalogue of all the qualities that George (1979) believed were a condition for success. Initially, most individuals will not possess all or most of them. Like any other profession, a developmental period of time will be necessary for the individual to become successful, and effective.

To develop these qualities, hard work, motivation, and formal and informal education will be necessary. Experience will become a valuable teacher. Rolemodeling other successful, effective supervisors will produce noticeable results. Desire and passion will motivate the individual to succeed where the more passive, timid individual will fail (Robbins, 1985).
Study, hard work, and on-the-job training will, in the long run, produce success and lead to a rewarding work experience.

2. LEADERSHIP

There are many good, effective supervisors in America and the world over. They work hard, produce results, earn economic and social rewards for their efforts, and live lives which can be considered admirable.

Among these individuals, there also exists those supervisors who are a cut above the rest. They too work hard, produce results, earn rewards, and yet have an elusive quality which makes them an uncommon lot. They are the supervisors who, because of special vision and extraordinary effort assume the role of leaders.

Leaders sometimes are not good supervisors. Some leaders may not be able to organize well, and do not possess the other skills listed above so that they can perform the other functions that supervisors are expected to perform. On the other hand, if a person aspires to become an extraordinary supervisor, it will be essential to possess many of the characteristics necessary to be a truly great leader. Many of us recognize a good leader, but cannot define precisely what makes one.

By observing outstanding leaders, it is possible to list a few of the qualities which they possess. In order to be a good leader, the supervisor will need to possess the following characteristics:

1. ***A desire to excel.*** A leader is never content with being second. He always wants to be out front. He is a self-starting individual who is willing to work long hours to achieve success.

2. ***A sense of responsibility.*** A leader is never afraid to seek and accept obligations to others. He always willingly discharges any responsibility he assumes.

3. ***A capacity for work.*** Good leaders are always willing to accept the demands of leadership success-- long hours and hard work.

4. ***A feel for good human relations.*** Leaders are always involved with their fellow workers, studying them, analyzing their needs and demands, and trying to understand their problems. This interest and ability to discover what their fellow workers need is in all probability the single most important characteristic of a good leader.

5. ***Need to exhibit a contagious enthus*iasm.** No one wants to follow a dull, uninspired leader. Enthusiasm is something like mob appeal--once we are caught up in it, we move along with it. And once workers are caught up in the web of enthusiasm for their jobs and their work, they take on a new sense of enthusiasm and commitment to the jobs they are asked to do.

6. ***A need to have a high sense of integrity.*** Any leader who succeeds has to be honest with himself and with his followers. He may fool some of the people for a while, but sooner or later a lack of honesty will force him out of a position of leadership. Few men who are insecure and undependable succeed as leaders (George, 1979, p. 23).

Poor leaders pass the blame along to others. They are self-centered. They ask employees to do things they would not do themselves. They are aloof, cool, unfriendly. They are the big "I" with their employees. They drag their feet. They so "Yes" and do not mean it. They agonize over decisions. They jump to conclusions.

Many people recognize that leadership is a part of supervision, and they sometimes fail to see that supervision is not the same thing as leadership. What is expected of a leader is to get others to follow him. A supervisor is asked to perform all of the functions associated with supervision in addition to being a leader. Although a strong leader may be a weak supervisor, a strong supervisor must be a good leader.

Leadership roles are often assumed by members of a work group. This is an informal position. He or she may be a leader today and be replaced tomorrow. Leadership in a group depends on what the group's objectives are. Sometimes the informal leader will be recognized for his or her specific abilities and then formally elevated to supervisor status. This is not often the case in Theory X management systems because there is a threat to the established power structure by the outsider. Sometimes this is amicably resolved if there is a need to include the outside leader. More often then not this person's skills are not fully utilized and he or she moves on to another organization or becomes demoralized and eventually loses his or her enthusiasm and falls out of a leadership role.

Whether he or she is an informal or formal leader, there are **Four Main Types of Leaders**:
1.   Dictatorial.
2.   Authoritarian.
3.   Democratic.
4.   Laissez-faire.

The **dictatorial** leader is a negative leader and holds threats of punishment, discharge, and fear over the heads of his employees to get them to do his will. He may get results in the short run, but over a period of time he cannot sustain such actions.

The **authoritarian** leader exercises strong control over his people. He or she resists help from others, and plays his or her "cards close to the chest" withholding information from the people and making them dependent on him or her for decisions. He or she is a strong "captain of the ship" and controls all coordination and interface between workers in achieving the group's goals.

The **democratic** leader solicits aid and advice from employees--trying to get them involved in work problems and their solutions. This is the type of leader whose group can function effectively even during his prolonged absences. The reason is because the employees in the group are used to working with problems and their solutions and are aware of the group's situation and progress. In the leader's absence, they can take over and move ahead.

The **laissez-faire** leader is not really much of a leader at all. He or she is a leader in name only, and his or her position of leadership is one decreed by upper management. This leader is more or less a figurehead with little or no power is virtually never listened to or respected by the employees (George, 1979, p. 27).

What type is the best? It depends upon the situation. In an emergency, an authoritarian type leader may be the best. If supervising a group of highly skilled self-starters, then the laissez faire leadership style may be best.

No one is a "born leader." Every person has the capacity to become a leader, but each will have to work hard at it. What capacities are necessary for a person who has some abilities to develop into a successful leader? George (1985) described these characteristics.

1. *Intelligence*. Leaders are usually a bit smarter or a bit more intelligent than their followers. This does not mean that a successful leader must have an excess of intelligence over his average follower. But it does mean that he is a bright and alert person with above average intelligence.
2. *Understanding*. A leader needs to have an understanding of and feeling for other people. Because a leader works with people and gets things done through the efforts of others, he must be accurately attuned to the feelings of others, to their goals, and to their problems. A good coaching leader should be sensitive to the values of the entire group in addition to those of the individuals.
3. *Social Activity*. A good leader needs to be active socially. He needs to participate actively in group functions. He needs to initiate actions for others and for the group as a whole.

4. ***Communication***. A good leader needs to be able to make his employees understand him and his ideas. He needs to be able to communicate messages accurately and clearly. If he can't communicate his "million dollar" idea, it is worthless.

5. ***Criticism***. A good leader can't let other people "get under his skin" with their criticisms. If he does, he's headed for failure. A good leader can and does take and welcome deserved criticism while shrugging off tactless, heavy-handed attacks from his adversaries (pp. 30-31).

Harrison (1989) captured and isolated the essence of leadership by studying some of the most famous leaders in Twentieth Century history. Here are a few selections describing leadership and certain themes related to it. They catalogue many aspects of the leader's position and activities. The people who made these comments certainly demonstrated in their lives the ability to "practice what they preached."

Ideals

The time is always right to do what is right.
Martin Luther King Jr.

Style

A true leader always keeps an element of surprise up his sleeve, which others cannot grasp but which keeps his public excited and breathless.
Charles de Gaulle

Vision

The empires of the future are empires of the mind.
Winston Churchill

Excellence

Don't be afraid to give your best to what seemingly are small jobs. Every time you conquer one it makes you that much stronger. If you do the little jobs well, the big ones tend to take care of themselves.

Dale Carnegie

Servant Leadership

The noblest service comes from nameless hands. And the best servant does his work unseen.

Oliver Wendell Holmes

Power

If a man can accept a situation in a place of power with the thought that it's only temporary, he comes out all right. But when he thinks he is the cause of the power, that can be his ruination.

Harry S. Truman

Responsibility

There are no office hours for leaders.

Cardinal Gibbons

Character

Good character is more to be praised than outstanding talent. Most talents are to some extent a gift. Good character, by contrast, is not given to us. We have to build it piece by piece--by thought, choice, courage, and determination.

John Luther

Honesty

I hope I shall possess firmness and virtue enough to maintain what I consider the most enviable of all titles, the character of an honest man.

George Washington

Integrity

The supreme quality for a leader is unquestionable integrity. Without it, no real success is possible, no matter whether it is on a section gang, a football field, in an army, or in an office.

Dwight D. Eisenhower

Enthusiasm

Every great and commanding moment in the annals of the world is the triumph of some enthusiasm.

Ralph Waldo Emerson

Positive Attitude

If you can dream it, you can do it.
Walt Disney

Courage

The ultimate measure of a man is not where he stands in moments of comfort and convenience, but where he stands at times of challenge and controversy.
Martin Luther King, Jr.

Determination

Most people give up just when they're about to achieve success. They quit on the one yard line. They give up at the last minute of the game one foot from a winning touchdown.
H. Ross Perot

Ambition

Show me a thoroughly satisfied man -- and I will show you a failure.
Thomas Edison

Setting the Example

Example is not the main thing in influencing others. It is the only thing.

Albert Schweitzer

Inspiring Employees

Techniques don't produce quality products or pick up the garbage on time; people do, people who care, people who are treated as creatively contributing adults.

Tom Peters

Communicating Effectively

When employees no longer believe that their manager listens to them, they start looking around for someone who will.

Ken Eye

Developing Subordinates

It is only as we develop others that we permanently succeed.

Harvey S. Firestone

Decision Making

Even though you're on the right track - you'll get run over if you just sit there.

Will Rogers, Jr.

Time Management

Most time is wasted, not in hours, but in minutes. A bucket with a small hole in the bottom gets just as empty as a bucket that is deliberately emptied.

Paul J. Meyer

Life's Lessons

As a man grows older...

...He values the voice of experience more and the voice of prophecy less.

...He finds more of life's wealth in the common pleasures - home, health and children.

...He thinks more about the work of men and less about their wealth.

...He begins to appreciate his own father a little more.

...He hurries less and usually makes more progress.

...He esteems the friendship of God a little higher.

Roy L. Smith

Failure

Failure is the opportunity to begin again more intelligently.

Henry Ford

Happiness

Most people are about as happy as they make up their minds to be.

Abraham Lincoln

Faith

Faith is the courage to face reality with hope.
Dr. Robert H. Schuller

Hope

We should not let our fears hold us back from pursuing our hopes.

John F. Kennedy

Love

Where there is love there is life.
Mohandas K. Gandhi

Kindness

Be kind. Remember everyone you meet is fighting a hard battle.

T.H. Thompson

Possibilities

Be brave enough to live creatively. The creative is the place where no one else has ever been. You have to leave the city of your comfort and go into the wilderness of your intuition. You can't get there by bus, only by hard work, risking, and by not quite knowing what you're doing. What you'll discover will be wonderful: yourself.
Alan Alda

Self-Development

Anyone who stops learning is old, whether at twenty or eighty. Anyone who keeps learning stays young. The greatest thing in life is to keep your mind young.
Henry Ford

Success

Success in life is nothing you do with what you gain in life or accomplish for yourself. It's what you do for others.
Danny Thomas

Requirements for Success

If one advances confidently in the direction of his dreams, and endeavors to live the life which he has imagined, he will meet with success unexpected in common hours.
Henry David Thoreau

The quotes from these famous leaders may inspire the supervisor who is striving to achieve a greater measure of success in his or her career. There is no easy path to greatness. Most of the individuals quoted were or are unique individuals who through their own initiative, intelligence, communication, and other skills served mankind as well as themselves. Their efforts forged the Twentieth Century into an age of unbelievable growth and development for mankind. Yet all were born, lived, and died on the earth like any other man or woman who came before them. As each leader passed on his or her torch to the next generation, new leaders emerged. As the 21st Century knocks at our front door, many of these leaders will be gone and it will be the province of this new generation to assume responsibility for the next century of leadership.

3. ESSENTIALS OF SUPERVISORY COMMUNICATION

Communication is simply the transfer of information and understanding from one person to another. It is successful only when a mutual understanding takes place; that is, when both the sender and receiver understand the message. Neither must agree with the idea. They must only understand it in order to consider their communication successful.

Sixty percent of communication is non-verbal and involves a pat on the back, drumming fingers, rocking in a chair, facial expressions, tapping the foot, and other such activities. Thirty-five percent of communication is the delivery. Tone of voice, voice volume, and rate of speech all enhance or detract from the messages being successfully sent and received. Only five percent of any communication process is the actual content of the message. The effective, successful, astute supervisor needs to become a master of both non-verbal and delivery methods which will enhance the communication process between supervisor and employee (Haney, 1986).

The tragedy is that many people, including mediocre supervisors, believe that the communication process is only the content. These individuals do not master the process and ultimately fail to succeed as supervisors. Those who do master these two communication areas generally rise to the top in their chosen fields.

In examining human communication, it is essential to understand that it is influenced by assumptions held by the communicators involved. Some of these assumptions are destructive and troublesome because (1) they are false and imply and inadequate, distorted view of the world, and (2) communicators are usually unaware that their evaluations and communications are being influenced by these assumptions.

As organizations grow larger and more complex, communicators, and especially supervisors, are challenged to respond to greater demands from their employees. The consequence of this is that organizations require greater competence on the part of its managers and key personnel than ever before.

In order to assist the supervisor in managing the communication process more effectively, Haney (1986) summarized the communication process and presented the following summary of how managers, supervisors, leaders, can be more effective in communicating with their employees.

1. **The Process of Perception.** The central premise is that what we experience is not reality but our perception of reality. Our willingness or inability to internalize this truism can readily lead us into defensive and self-destructive behavior. We are challenged to recognize that our "reality" is subjective, partial, unique, and subject to bias - and to ascertain accurately the perceptions of others.

2. **The Frame of Reference and the Self-Image.** The frame of reference concept is likened to a stained-glass window in one's solitary confinement cell. The major lens of this window is one's self-image. A valid self-concept is essential if one is to deal effectively with others.

3. **The Exceptionally Realistic Self-Image (ERSI).** Among the advantages that a person with an ERSI enjoys are the liberation of energy that would otherwise be required for self-image protection, the ease of maintaining an ERSI, the prerequisites for developing skills for reading others and screening inputs, and the selection of realistic personal goals. A game plan for attaining an ERSI is:

    a. Make an earnest commitment to discover yourself.

    b. Recognize and reduce your defenses against valid feedback.

    c. Receive and evaluate the external and internal cues.

External cues are those we receive from others. Internal cues are those we receive from ourselves.

4.   ***Motivation and Communication***. "The easiest thing of all is to deceive oneself; for what a man wishes he generally believes to be true." Demosthenes. Motivation causes people to pursue different goals. In understanding what motivates an individual, the supervisor can more effectively communicate with him or her if this basic understanding exists between them.

5.   ***The Process of Communication***. Communication process involves encoding, transmitting, medium, receiving, and decoding. Encoding and decoding are the most subtle, least understood, and most neglected phases of the process. The insidious role of fallacious, unconsciously held assumptions is underscored as being the root of most communication problems between supervisors and employees and vice versa.

6.   ***The Inference-Observation Confusion***. The inference-observation confusion occurs when one somehow acts upon inference as if it were an accurate observation. One of the key reasons that we often find it easy to substitute inference for observations is that our statements of inference can be readily confused with statements of observation. There is nothing in our language (grammar, spelling, pronunciation, syntax, and so on), that distinguishes between the two statements. A four-step procedure for coping with the inference observation confusion is:

    1.   Detect the inference.
    2.   Calculate the probability that the inference is correct.
    3.   Get more data - if the risk is a poor one.
    4.   Recalculate the risk.

Creativity and decisiveness are not incompatible with inference awareness. Creativity can be facilitated when one is conscious of inferring. The quality of decisions can be enhanced by inference awareness. It is not the avoidance of inferring (risk-taking) but the awareness of it.

7.   **Bypassing**. Bypassing occurs when communicators miss each other with their meanings either by using the same word while meaning different things or by using different words while meaning the same thing. Resulting in false disagreements (or agreements), bypassing can sometimes be innocuous, even humorous. Underlying bypassing is the supposition that words mean the same to the other person as they do to me. This belief is supported by two insidious fallacies; that words have **mono-usage**; that words have **meanings**. To guard against bypassing, the communicator can supplant these assumptions with two others that represent much more adequately the relation between words or meanings: (1) most words, with the exception of some technical terms, are used in more than one way; (2) meanings exist not in words but only in the people who speak, hear, write, and read them, the people, who fix the variables--that is, assign meanings to words.

8.   **Allness**. Allness is a sort of evaluational disease. It occurs when one unconsciously assumes that it is possible to know and to say everything about something; that what one is saying (or writing or thinking) covers all there is (or all that is important) about a subject. When we fail to realize that we are abstracting, that is, leaving out details, we are in distinct danger of believing that we have left out nothing--nothing of consequence, at any rate. Arrogance, intolerance of other view points, and close-mindedness are frequent consequences of such false assurance. To intensify our awareness of abstracting and thus avoid allness, Haney suggested we should:

1. Cultivate the humility to concede that we can never say or know everything about anything.
2. Recognize that abstracting is inevitable when we talk, listen, and so on, for then we would be more likely to improve the quality of our abstractions, be empathetic, and be creative and less inhibited by past practices.
3. "Remember the etc." a simple yet effective device.
4. Free ourselves from the insularity of an "all-wall."

9. ***Indiscrimination***. Indiscrimination occurs when one fails to recognize differences among the similarities. The frequent result is that one reacts to blacks, police officers, politicians, business executives, lawyers, Jews, and so forth as if they were all identical--or at least enough alike to preclude any important differences. The basic device for warding off dogmatic, unreasonable indiscriminations is the "Which Index"--black 1 is not the same as black 2, and so on.

10. ***Polarization***. Polarization is the result of the confusion of contraries. It is the tendency to evaluate and communicate in black-and-white terms when shades of gray would be more appropriate. This pattern of communication is dangerous enough on the interpersonal level, but on the national and international levels, it can be catastrophic. To cope with the pendulum effect, it is helpful to regard differing perceptions as the consequence of differing conditioning and to concede that in complicated problems no one (including ourselves) has the one complete and incontestable solution.

11. ***The Frozen Evaluation***. The frozen evaluation generally occurs when one assumes non-change. It tends to occur when one unconsciously believes that the way it is now is the way it has always been--or always will be. This can be a troublesome and dangerous premise because literally nothing (especially human beings) remains the same. We can keep ourselves alert to the process nature of life by habitually When-Indexing (dating) out thoughts and statements. Man (1973), after all, is not the same as Man (1993).

12. ***Intentional Orientation***. Intentional orientation invites trouble, confusion, and conflict (1) because often our maps (one's child care theories and notions, for example) inadequately and fallaciously represent the territory (the flesh-and-blood child's feelings and behavior) and (2) because we may be unaware that we are dealing primarily with these maps and not with the respective territories that they represent. The basic remedy for diminishing the destructive effects of intentional orientation is to "get intentional." That is, develop a readiness to go out and examine the territory rather than be content to be deluded by one's often spurious maps. The byword of extensionality is to look first--then talk.

13. ***Pointing and Associating***. Among the ways we use words are these: (1) simply to point to, or call attention to, what we representing by the words and (2) to evoke associations (memories, feelings) for what we are referring to. When one is unaware that words may be used for these dual purposes, there is the possibility of a number of miscommunication patterns, including the "pointing-association" confusion; name calling; and associative by-passing.

14. **Blindering**. If in defining a problem, I am unaware of leaving out details, I am in danger of becoming blindered - of unconsciously permitting a narrowed perception to restrict my attack of the problem. The basic correctives are (1) to remember that definitions inevitably involve the exclusion of details (perhaps crucial ones) and (2) to recognize and remove your blinders.

15. **Undelayed Reactions**. Some undelayed reactions, such as reflex responses, are largely unavoidable, harmless, and even self-protective. Others, such as many reflex-like responses, may be highly useful when they have been properly conditioned and employed--the numerous actions of driving an automobile, for example. But some reflex-like responses--for instance, those manifested in fear and rage--are often destructive. It is the latter that should be controlled if we are to avoid contributing to the harm of ourselves and others (pp. 555-559).

This is a comprehensive explanation of the common communication errors which supervisors are prone to commit. The management of the communication process is the most important aspects of all the supervisor's functions. In order to communicate effectively, he or she must not only be able to encode, but decode. This means the supervisor must be an active listener.

The supervisor must not only listen to the words an employee sends, but also must listen to the meaning the employee is placing on the words. Listening is hard work. Listening with "one ear" is not very effective. Some of the basic rule for effective listening are:
1. Be interested in the message.
2. Resist distractions.
3. Don't let personal biases turn you off.
4. Try to understand the words and the implied message.
5. Work hard to understand difficult ideas or materials.
6. Don't hesitate to ask questions (Haney, 1986, pp. 38-39).

These are general principles. Specific skills which need to be practiced are:

1. Looking and acting interested.
2. Mirroring.
3. Paraphrasing.
4. Repeating.
5. Verification.
6. Affirming.
7. Silence or pausing to wait.
8. Touch.
9. Pacing (Haney, 1986).

All organizations transfer information to employees in two ways: formal and informal channels.

Formal channels usually follow a company's organizational lines of authority from the top man to the bottom echelons. In theory, there is a two-way flow, but in practice this does not always occur. The communication is often sidetracked or stopped. A supervisor may feel that a certain piece of information should not be passed on up to his boss because (1) he doesn't want to bother him with trivia; or (2) he may feel it would not reflect well on his ability as a supervisor. Upward communications are usually questions, complaints, or grievances, and many supervisors consciously tend to stop the flow of such communications.

Informal channels of communication, variously known as the "grapevine," the "rumor mill," "scuttlebutt," always exist. These forms develop as a result of employees working together and talking about their jobs. News which comes from these sources is typically more gossip than truth, is unreliable, unconfirmed, and unauthenticated. Despite these characteristics, it draws people like a magnet.

These forms of communication are not effective for supervisors. The effective supervisor tells news to a person directly. To stifle the flow of rumors, a supervisor needs to answer all questions as promptly and truthfully as possible. If employees can be certain they will receive accurate information if they ask for it, the "grapevine" will dry up and wither.

Communication breaks down because barriers often exist that hamper or distort the flow of communication between people. These breakdowns frequently can (1) cost time and money to the company, (2) cause employees to lose work, (3) create misunderstandings, (4) cause a breakdown in team effort, and (5) seriously damage morale.

Telephone conversations can often cause misunderstandings. There is no way to read the non-verbal communication the employee is receiving from the supervisor. Not receiving communication face-to-face can prevent an employee from asking questions related to what the employee is seeing.

Sometimes a supervisor may prejudice a person. He may already have his mind made up about an employee's ability, and he may let this prejudgment show. He or she might say, for example, "You probably won't understand this, but I'll try to explain it to you anyway." The employee, knowing that the supervisor has no confidence in his or her capacity to understand, might therefore make little effort to understand what the supervisor is saying.

A supervisor may block communication by saying to his or her employee, "Where did you get such a wild idea?" Even a good idea and communication would probably be stifled with such an introduction.

Age can act as a barrier to communication. An older supervisor may have a crew-cut hairstyle, and the young employee may have long hair and an earring. They both understand the words that are being spoken, but because they are alienated by the "generation gap" as expressed in their personal styles, neither one accepts the other person for what he or she is, and communications is hampered.

Physical disabilities and inadequacies need to be considered when communicating with others. A person who is hard of hearing may have difficulty hearing what is being said. He or she may even feel that the supervisor is talking in a low tone of voice to frustrate him or her.

What are some of the easiest strategies to invoke in order to overcome communications barriers? Consider these following actions steps to enhance the process of communication.

1. **Face-to-face talks are always better than other forms of communication.** Talking directly to a person enables him or her to ask questions to clarify what is being said during the conversation.

2. **Simple, clear, clean-cut language does a lot to break down barriers to understanding.** Long, complicated sentences and words are sure to lead to confusion.

3. **Repetition is another way to overcome communication barriers.** Repeating the message several times using different words can aid comprehension.

4. **Trying to place yourself in the other fellow's shoes can lead to greater communication.** In the process of empathizing with another's feelings, opinions, and attitudes, supervisors can communicate in ways that might surprise the employee.

5. **Being genuinely concerned about the welfare of the other person and about the possible effect that the communication will have on him.**

6. **When possible, choose a physical location that will help and not hinder communication.** Talking over a problem in a quiet office free from noise and distractions and without the phone ringing constantly is much different than from talking in an atmosphere where there are a host of distractions (George, 1979, pp. 42-43).

The supervisor's role in the communication process is essential. Although every person in any organization is responsible for some aspect of communication, the supervisor is charged with maintaining a good climate for communications with his or her employees. He or she is responsible for seeing that employees understand each other, their jobs, and the organization's goals and objectives. The supervisor is the linking chain between departments, and he or she must realize that the total communication climate in a company is no stronger than the weakest supervisor.

A first-line supervisor is responsible for good communications and understanding within his or her unit. Most supervisors will explain that poor communications cause more problems than any other single item.

Communications that are effectively made can have a healthy and positive effect on the climate and production of an organization. The supervisor needs to be a better communicator than the average employee because his or her scope of influence is greater. In order to accomplish this, supervisors need to always be informed and ready to communicate with employees. When mysteries arise in any organization and the supervisor is not aware of their genesis, communication problems are sure to arise.

To gain his or her employee's confidence, the supervisor needs to be consistent in his or her communications practices. He or she should not say one thing today and another thing tomorrow. This confidence between supervisor and employer can and will ensure good communication between them.

Communications and orders easily flow down the line, but information from the employees upward also needs to go up the line without being sidetracked. Many supervisors do not realize how difficult it may be for an employee to communicate with them. Whatever the reason, the supervisor must take this into consideration.

Another barrier to upward communications is the fact that the supervisor controls the employee's job and pay. The employee may be hesitant to say something that may in some way affect his or her job. Since his or her job is dependent on the supervisor, this may cause him or her to hesitate to "speak up" to the supervisor. Supervisors need to be aware of the existence of this difficulty and make every effort to make it easier for the worker to "speak his mind." The upward flow of communications is hampered and in many cases is stopped altogether.

A supervisor cannot know too much about employee communications. He or she supervises his employees by communicating with them, and the skill with which he or she communicates will be reflected in the skill with which he or she manages. Depending on the person, the situation, and the information to be covered, supervisors communicate in different ways to different people.

Supervisors often over-communicate. Communicate enough to let employees know everything necessary but not so much that they will "tune out" old blabbermouth when talking. Talk about the things they want to know about and are interested in like their jobs, their pay, the things that affect them at work. It may be necessary to avoid controversial non-work subjects like politics and religion.

The effects of good communication within an organization cannot be easily measured, but they are reflected in several ways. An employee's attitude toward the company and his or her job will be improved as will be his morale, his cooperation, and his job satisfaction. With a healthier communication climate, a similar improvement in the work climate will develop. Good communication will not make all things come true, but when a healthy attitude toward work and a free climate of communication exists, it is natural that an organization will experience an overall improvement in its communication, both up and down the line of supervision.

4. SUPERVISORS AND HUMAN RELATIONS PRACTICES

Practicing good human relations means applying the "Golden Rule." It is also the application of psychology to people; that is, winning friends and influencing people. It can be considered an ethical approach to personnel problems. In practicing good human relations supervisors work toward getting employees to work together harmoniously, productively, and cooperatively to achieve economic as well as social satisfaction. The supervisor must motivate employees to want to do productive and satisfying jobs. It is a key part of effective human relations - to motivate people.

Supervisors must remember employees who work for them are members of the organization for only part of their lives. They are family members, members of churches, clubs, and citizens of a community. Understanding this, the effective supervisor must recognize that he or she cannot change an employee merely by bringing him into a plant, having him punch a clock or sign in, and assigning him a place to work. Even though he works for the organization, he still has his own personal problems and attitudes that come with him to job, and he will continue to be influenced by his associations with other organizations.

Individual differences affect the supervisor's role. Each employee comes to the job with a predetermined set of requirements that the job may fulfill like status or the need to belong to a group. Men and women sometimes look at a job differently. Women may see employment as a transitory period in their lives as they prepare for married life and motherhood. This was characteristic of women for the period of human history up until this past decade. Women's' roles are rapidly changing and the previous statement does not seem to be currently accurate. Most families now have two "bread winners."

Age influences individuals. Older employees are more apt to be security-conscious than younger ones. They are prone to maintain their present situations rather than transferring like younger employees to other positions with unknown opportunities.

George (1970) encouraged supervisors to remember several facts about individuals which make managing much easier and more effective:

1. **Remember that all of us are different.** We each have our own individual minds, our own thoughts, our own ideas about life, our own wants.

2. **Remember that when you are working with a person, you are working with a whole person.** You might wish you could employ him as a hired hand, but you can't. As a supervisor, you need to remember that every employee is different and that you must work with him or her as whole people.

3. **Remember that all normal behavior by an individual is caused behavior.** It is caused by individual needs or wants. Employees are not motivated by what you think they ought to do and have but by what they think they ought to do and have. Often supervisors think that things that another person wants and the reasons he wants them may appear foolish. To him, they are important, real needs. These needs cause the behavior with which you will be dealing.

4. **Remember that people are not machines to be knocked about and thrown out when you are through with them.** As human beings, people need and ought to be treated with dignity and respect. No matter what a person's job is, no matter how "low" you may think it is, he or she deserves to be and should be shown the proper respect for his or her choice of jobs and his or her own abilities (pp. 320-21).

Supervisors get things done through other people. Thus, a supervisor's effectiveness will be measured by how productive his or her employees are. To deny a supervisor's success is dependent upon employees is to deny reality. Employees generally want to please their employee for a variety of reasons. If a supervisor can discover what motivates each and every one of them and somehow provide each with whatever it takes, he or she will be eminently successful. Remembering that the employee will only work as hard as he or she chooses to work, finding what makes him or her work harder is essential. The effective supervisor is the one who can create a work climate in which the employee **willingly** strives to do his or her best, each and every day, throughout the duration of his or her employment with the organization.

In order to understand employees and create a human relations environment in which all differences are celebrated, the supervisor must first understand him or herself.

Haney (1986) encouraged managers to develop an **Exceptionally Realistic Self-Image** (ERSI). When a supervisor begins to know him or herself, he or she has taken the first step toward understanding "self." The supervisor who realizes that he or she has certain attitudes about dress, working fast or slow, and how a supervisor should behave, soon realizes that others have similar ideas. The supervisor with an ERSI will be in a better position to treat employees fairly and justly.

Understanding self means looking at strengths as well as weaknesses. It is often easy to see strong points, but the budding supervisor will have to work harder to see weak points. In realizing shortcomings, the supervisor will be in a position to try and control them and thereby become a better one in the long run.

An effective supervisor must work at empathizing with his or her employees. He or she needs to make this so much a part of him or herself that it comes as easily as shaking hands. It should be so much a part of him or her that he or she will be able to quickly settle a dispute, prevent a grievance from arising, or shed new light on a tough problem.

The better a supervisor knows his or her employees, knows about the size of his family, the age of his children, what their names are, where they go to school, what their accomplishments are, the better he or she will know and understand the employee.

Supervisors often find they spend much of their time with a group of employees. This may be a formal group, such as a clinical team of which the supervisor is a member, or it may be an informal group, such as a bowling team, or a group that gets together to play cards or watch movies on the weekends.

Groups differ greatly in their attraction they hold for members. One peculiarity of groups that the supervisor should recognize is that the people who are most vocal and try hardest to influence the other members of the group are usually the ones who are most willing to accept the opinions of others. This seems contradictory, but it is a characteristic of the behavior of employees in groups. If one employee wants desperately to influence others, if he wants to be the leader and spokesman, the he will be willing to accept the views and suggestions of the other employees so that he can "lead them." The stronger the ties of the group and the more cohesive it is, the more the rule holds true. If it didn't work this way, then the employee who was vocal and said things the group did not agree with would soon be cut off from the group if he did not accept their views (George, 1970).

All humans have certain basic needs that they want fulfilled. Some basic human needs that are similar for all people are food, clothing, shelter, self-respect, recognition, and self-esteem. Individual employees place different weight on different needs. A starving man will place a greater emphasis on obtaining food. A man with plenty of food but little clothing will seek out clothing to meet his needs. If a supervisor knows what an employee's needs are, he or she will be much more successful in meeting those needs. The simplest way to ascertain what an employee's needs are is to simply ask him or her. It is not a complicated matter to be direct and inquire not once, but on an on-going basis. Needs change, and what an employee needs, or wants today, may change tomorrow. The effective supervisor considers the dynamic nature of his or her employees and stays tuned to the changing needs of employees.

George (1979) studied the basic wants and desires of the average employee and listed them as follows:

1. Fair pay.
2. Recognition as an individual.
3. Opportunity for advancement.
4. Interesting work in a good place to work.
5. Acceptance by the group.
6. Good and just leadership.

What weight placed on these needs and desires by various workers will differ. The effective supervisor will recognize these and other individual needs and the different weights that each employee places on them.

Practicing good human relations does not mean that everybody will be all smiles and happiness. There will be problems, but practicing human relations enables the supervisor to work around the difficulties that the problems present. George (1970) suggested the following human relations practices that the effective supervisor should aim for in his or her work:

1. Peace among your employees.
2. Openness and understanding.
3. A friendly air between workers.
4. Employees expecting and receiving a fair and just hearing and decision (p. 23).

In order to determine how successful a supervisor is in using human relations skills, George (1979) created the following **Human Relations Scale** to measure skill levels. The scale can be found on the next page.

HUMAN RELATIONS SKILLS SCALE

Directions: Your job is to supervise the employees working for you in your department. In doing this, you will have an opportunity to test all of your human relations skills. Answer the following questions honestly to see how you are on the human relations scale. Give yourself 4 points for each "yes" answer. A score of 80 or better places you high on the scale of practicing good human relations with your employees.

1. Do you know each employee well?
2. Do you talk to your employees about their homes, their hobbies, and their families?
3. Do you tell your employees how they are getting along on the job?
4. Do you give them credit when credit is due?
5. Do you tell them in advance about changes that will affect them?
6. Are you open-minded? Do you ask for suggestions?
7. Do you respect all jobs and make them seem important?
8. Are you courteous in your treatment of your employees?
9. Are you honest, impartial, and fair in your dealings and judgment?
10. Do you treat your employees with dignity and make them feel that they are a part of the company group--that they belong?
11. Are you generally cheerful?
12. Do you try to be a good listener?
13. Do you always consider every complaint?
14. Are you equally strict (or lenient) with all employees?
15. Do you praise good work and criticize poor work?
16. Can you say "no" to an employee without making him feel antagonistic toward you?
17. Can you empathize--see the other fellow's point of view?
18. Can you give clear and easily understood orders?
19. Do you explain why changes have to be made?

20. Do you do everything you honestly can to get workers promoted or transferred to better jobs?
21. Do your employees come to you freely with job or personal problems?
22. Do you try to explain each employee's job and its relation to the whole company in order to show the employee that his job is important?
23. Can you freely accept personal criticism from your employees about how you operate as a supervisor without getting upset?
24. Do your employees respond positively when you talk to them about doing a better job?
25. Do you know yourself as well as you know your employees?

Your Score:

5. SUPERVISION AND EMPLOYEE MORALE

Motivation in any endeavor is a function of the morale of the individual. Motivation can be based on needs and wants, and morale, like motivation, is a state of mind, or how the individual feels about things. When morale is high, the individual generally feels good about things, optimistic, enthusiastic, and energetic. Low morale produces opposing feelings. Many things affect morale like health, the work environment, family experiences, supervision, the company the individual works for, and the condition of the individual's community, state, nation, and the world. It is not a result of a single attitude or feeling, but a combination of several factors.

Morale specifically related to the work place will certainly affect an employee's willingness to work. It varies based upon how intensely the individual employee feels about work and the work place. Some employees work 100% of the time, and generally their morale is very high. Others take a take-it-or-leave-it attitude. Their indifference is difficult to interpret, but certainly affects their performance.

Individual differences affect morale. Those who believe that "idle hands are the devil's workshop" tend to approach work with vigor and a positive frame of mind. However, they are not happy at work and do not display good morale unless they are working at a meaningful job. If they consider themselves to be "underemployed" then they may find work distasteful and put a high premium on leisure time.

Does supervision affect morale?
Yes.

The way an individual is supervised has a direct bearing on their morale. Morale is always present. Sometimes it is high and sometimes it is low, but it is never absent. On a continuum, there exists some point between extremely good and very poor.

Supervisors cannot use their authority to order employees to have high morale. It cannot be purchased. The only thing the effective supervisor can do is to create a healthy climate in which high morale can develop. High morale develops out of good human relations, good employee motivation, respect for the individual, recognition of individual differences, good supervision, good communication, understanding, counseling, and other effective supervisory practices.

Morale varies from day to day. It can spread in a contagious fashion, but can erode just as quickly. The effective supervisor then, needs to exert daily energy to maintain a satisfactory level of morale among employees.

Employees are individually affected by the morale the effective supervisor develops. The effects of good morale are these:
1.   Work is a pleasure not a chore.
2.   Working with others is a source of satisfaction rather than a source of ill feelings.
3.   Employees are usually pleased with their jobs and have confidence in their abilities to get their work done.

In attempting to understand what affects morale, the supervisor must begin with the individual. Some things cannot be changed. An employee with family problems may experience a period of low morale. Although the supervisor cannot change these conditions, he or she can be aware of their existence and do whatever he or she can to ameliorate them. Helping the employee to "get it off his chest" whatever is upsetting him. Encouraging the employee to talk about personal issues does not eliminate them, but certainly can aid in making the employee feel as if the supervisor understands and may even empathize with them.

Employee morale is influenced by factors that are within supervision's control. These include job security, adequate compensation for work performed, working conditions, interesting work, and recognition for a job done well. These factors affect morale and neglecting them may cause a decrease in it.

How and what the supervisor does and says directly affects employee morale. The supervisor's giving directions and leading have a direct effect on employee morale. If a supervisor loses his or her temper, shows a condition of fear, indicates a sense of insecurity about him or herself, employee morale will be affected. The effective supervisor needs to lead in a positive way. He or she needs to seek out an employees' help to correct an error that has been made rather than to try and hid a problem. Confident leadership begets confident employees and creates a work climate where morale can be high.

High morale does not always ensure high productivity. High morale can place an employee in a frame of mind to increase productivity. If good supervision and good working conditions are present, morale will be affected and productivity generally will increase.

Can morale be measured? Yes. The following are examples of the kinds of questions the effective supervisors can ask their employees to ascertain what morale climate exists.

MORALE OPINION SURVEY

1.   Do you like to work for this company?

☐   Dislike.

☐   It is OK.

☐   Like the Company.

☐   Very happy working here.

2.   Does your supervisor keep you informed about what's going on?

☐   Never

☐   Rarely

☐   About half the time.

☐   Yes, always.

3.   Does your supervisor listen to your complaints or grips and handle them quickly and fairly?

☐   No. Very unsatisfactory.

☐   He tries but doesn't do enough.

☐   He handles them well.

By analyzing the answers, supervisors can tell how employees feel about their jobs, what parts of their jobs they feel strongly about, and how they feel about their supervisors. Morale surveys give the employee the opportunity to say what is on his or her mind. They permit vertical communication to take place freely. These surveys are important because they indicate to an employee that the company and its supervisors are interested in his or her opinions--that the company cares.

George (1979) maintained that "Morale surveys have another advantage: they focus management's attention on morale and its importance to the company, making supervisors 'morale-conscious'" (p. 71).

What are some of the signs of low morale? Though this is not an all-inclusive list, here are some of them:

1. High employee turnover.
2. No respect for supervisors.
3. Low productivity.
4. Excessive waste.
5. Large number of grievances.
6. High number of accidents.
7. General lack of cooperation.
8. Poor quality of production.
9. Low regard for the company.
10. Excessive lateness.
11. Excessive sick leaves.
12. Leaving work early.
13. Long lunch periods.
14. Excessive one-day absences.
15. Excessive rumor-mongering (George, 1970, p. 74).

The effective supervisor needs to keep these signs of low morale in mind and should take immediate steps to change the conditions and help change the attitude causing the low state of morale.

What can a supervisor do to help build morale? George (1979) suggested the following strategies to accomplish this:

1. Develop an understanding and appreciation of the employee as a person;

2.   Be sure that his pay is just and fair and in line with pay for comparable jobs in the community;
3.   Look after the general working conditions making sure of comfort, safety, and cleanliness;
4.   Periodically talk with each employee about his or her job performance, his progress, and the opportunities that might lie ahead for him;
5.   Point out his or her need (if any) for additional skills, training, or education in order for him to take advantage of future opportunities (p. 75).

The closer a supervisor is with his or her employees the more effective he or she will be in raising and maintaining the level of morale in his or her department.

It is as simple as that.

6. SUPERVISION AND PROBLEM SOLVING

Supervision and managing employees is the job of making decisions-decisions about hiring new employees, about promotions, about training, about equipment, about productivity, about communications, about disciplining, about morale, and so on. Supervisors are paid primarily for one thing and that is to make sound decisions. To do an effective job, the supervisor needs to make good decisions because making good ones is the essence of good supervision and the key to success as a supervisor.

Some supervisors make decisions based purely on reason, logic, what makes sense. These individuals do not often take employees' individual feelings into consideration, and at times, this can lead to problems. His or her main concern is to get the job done and taking into feelings into account gets in the way.

On the other extreme is the supervisor who takes weeks to decide an answer that should have taken a few hours at most. He never gets excited, puts off taking action, and tells his or her employees that things will work out OK in a few days.

Keirsey and Bates (1984) described these two different temperaments as the **T**hinking and **F**eeling personality types. The **T** supervisor uses logic and reason and does not consider peoples' feelings in making a decision; the **F** type considers feelings in lieu of logic and reason, but is often inept in being able to make a decision in a timely fashion.

Between these two extremes is the middle-of-the-road supervisor who hesitates to makes decisions that will upset anyone. He or she wants to be everyone's friend and cannot bring him or herself to make a decision that will be against anyone's wishes. This type of supervisor gives answers that are watered-down compromises that seldom upset others and seldom solve any problems.

There is also the "research" type supervisor who refuses to make a decision until all facts are thoroughly reviewed. Sometimes the facts are not all available so decisions are not made, or it takes so long to get "all the facts" that the opportunity to take action has passed. There are worriers who agonize over every decision, and there are the shy and timid types who never have the courage to face a problem head on. There are the one-of-a-kind type that cause most of the difficulties that supervisors experience by not considering enough facts and acting indiscriminately.

Effective decision making is the first step in problem solving. There are five steps in the traditional problem solving process. Many individuals solve problems so unconsciously they are not aware that the steps even exist. These steps are:

1. Accurately define what the problem is;
2. Brainstorm for solutions, choices, options;
3. Pick the solution, choice, or option that seems to be the best;
4. Implement the solution, choice, or option;
5. Evaluate to see if it worked.

If a supervisor is not alert for problems, problems will certainly arise. Not clearly defining the problem can lead to a lot of energy being squandered on actions which produce no meaningful results. Systematically analyzing the problem and then brainstorming for options can lead to more effective management of problem-laden situations. Solving the problem once a solution, choice, or option is picked is, in fact, the easiest part of the entire process.

Can brainstorming really work? Yes, because the "ten-heads-are-better-than-one" approach can provide many solutions not available to the single problem solver. Such an activity does not constrict the supervisor to thinking barriers that limit effective action.

deBono (1985) teaches an entire thinking technology which presents new and unique ways to approach thinking related to problem solving. His **PMI** thinking tool is "so simple" deBono maintains that it is almost unlearnable because everyone thinks he or she uses it anyway. The letters are chosen to give a nicely pronounceable abbreviation so that individuals can ask themselves or others, to "do a PMI."

P	stands for Plus or the good points.
M	stands for Minus or the bad points.
I	stands for Interesting or the interesting points.

The **PMI** is an attention-directing tool. In doing a *PMI* the individual deliberately directs his or her attention first toward the Plus points, then toward the Minus points, and finally toward the Interesting points. This is done in a very deliberate and disciplined manner over a period of about 2-3 minutes in all.

deBono (1985) used this example to demonstrate the **PMI** method with a group of educators. He asked a group of 30 students aged 10-12 to tell him what they thought of the idea of each of them receiving $5 a week just for going to school. Most loved the idea and began to tell him what they would do with the money. All of them loved the idea. deBono then explained the **PMI** thinking method and asked them to use it in regard to the $5 suggestion. At the end of the exercise the class was asked again if they liked the idea. Whereas 30 out of 30 liked it at first, now 29 out of 30 had completely reversed their view and now disliked the idea. What deBono noted was that using this very simple scanning tool, used by the youngsters themselves, had brought about change.

In Practical Thinking, deBono (1971) wrote that "everyday thinking is what fills in the time when you are neither asleep nor dead. Just as you notice a car engine only when it is not running smoothly, so you become aware of everyday thinking when it is not running smoothly." deBono regarded thinking as a skill rather than a gift and maintained accepting this notion was the first step towards doing something to improve the skill.

deBono (1976) suggested that an individual must learn to think in order to be an effective problem solver. He defined thinking as "the deliberate exploration of experience for a purpose," and that purpose may be decision-making, planning, problem solving, judgement, and action.

Sometimes, deBono (1970) hypothesized, lateral thinking is necessary to solve new and unique problems. He defined this type of thinking as being concerned with the generation of ideas. He described lateral thinking as different than vertical thinking which moves forward by sequential steps each of which must be justified. Lateral thinking is not a substitute for vertical thinking, but both are required and complementary. Lateral thinking is generative; vertical thinking is selective. Supervisors need to utilize both types if they are to be effective in problem solving. In defining the need for the use of lateral thinking, deBono wrote:

> The purpose of thinking is to collect information and to make the best possible use of it. Because of the way the mind works to create fixed concept patterns we cannot make the best use of new information unless we have some means for restructuring the old patterns and bringing them up to date. Our traditional methods of thinking teach us how to refine such patterns and establish their validity. But we shall always make less than the best use of available information unless we know how to create new patterns and escape with providing or developing concept patterns. Vertical thinking is concerned with proving or developing concept patterns. Lateral thinking is concerned with restructuring such patterns (insight) and provoking new ones (creativity). Lateral and vertical thinking are complementary. Skill in both (for supervisors) is necessary. Yet the emphasis in education and business has always been exclusively on vertical thinking. The need for lateral thinking arises from the limitations of the behavior of the mind as a self-maximizing memory system (p. 13).

Our traditional YES/NO thinking system, deBono (1972) wrote is immensely effective in the second stage of thinking: that is in making the best use of fixed ideas. Unfortunately the system is not much use in the first stage of thinking: that is the perception stage which involves creating new ideas and new ways of looking at things. Just as NO is the basic tool of logical thinking so a new word **PO** is suggested as the basic tool for the first stage of thinking. Logical YES/NO thinking is based on judgement, but **PO** thinking is based on movement. Both types of thinking are necessary. But we must realize that logic is unlikely to solve those problems which need a new idea for their solution.

PO is a new word. It is a magic word. "It will do all you want it to do," deBono (1972) wrote, "if you believe in it. As with all magic, the more you believe the better it works. The more you invest in it, the more you get out of it. But there is no dogma you have to accept before you can use **PO**. It is a simple word and all you have to believe in is its use. The use of **PO** can easily be described as a prompt to use when a problem arises. For instance: Employees are preparing to form a union to support them in addressing grievances against the company. The supervisor invokes **PO**: What are the strategies necessary for the organization to undertake to assist the employees in forming their union?

PO, deBono (1972) wrote, is a deliberately invented thinking tool. **PO** is:

1. A skill which can be learned and practiced just as an individual learns to drive a car, cook, or play golf. It is like a reverse gear in a car. Without a reverse gear in a car the individual can get blocked in the first blind alley you come to. Without **PO** in our thinking process, unless the individual is following a well-known circular track leading nowhere.

2. A change tool directly concerned with new ideas, new approaches, and the escape from concept prisons.

3. A thinking tool that is as basic to creative thinking as NO is to logical thinking.

4.   A tool that can unlock latent creative reserve. Most people are unable to use their creative reserves, because there is no key with which to unlock the door that has been locked by traditional educational rigidity.

5.   A laxative for those who have a constipated minds that they wish to be free.

6.   Directly related to humor because the individual can go beyond the obvious to seek new ways of looking at things. The three intellectual ages of man could be described as follows:
0 - 5   years: the age of WHY?
5 - 10   years: the age of WHY NOT?
10- 75 + years: the age of BECAUSE?

7.   Acts to keep the age of WHY NOT going alongside the age of BECAUSE which society does need in order to have competence. In adults, **PO** can serve to resurrect the child's creative way of looking at things.

8.   Perfectly reasonable - but completely illogical. We have been trained to believe that the absence of logic is chaos, confusion, and even madness, but it is not. **PO** is certainly illogical, but nevertheless, very reasonable. We have been brainwashed over the ages to believe that logic is the only way of handling ideas in order to reach a useful result.

9.   Acts to break down established patterns, and introduce discontinuity. Its main function is to act as an anti-arrogance and anti-dogmatism device.

10.   Accepted or rejected by each individual dependent upon each one's needs (pp. 23-25).

In a later text, deBono (1985) wrote how even individuals who understand vertical, lateral, **PO**, and other types of thinking processes he wrote about can get stuck. He described a method called the **Six Thinking Hats** to assist individuals to move from one method of thinking to another. "Putting on" a hat focuses thinking. "Switching hats" redirects thinking. With the different parts of the thinking process thus clearly defined, discussion between individuals can be better focused and more productive.

What are the hats? deBono described them as such:

1. WHITE: facts, figures, and objective information.
2. RED: emotions and feelings.
3. BLACK: logical negative thoughts.
4. YELLOW: positive constructive thoughts.
5. GREEN: creativity and ideas.
6. BLUE: control of the other hats and thinking steps.

If dealing with individuals, a supervisor can arrest thinking which is blocking communication, tangential, or destructive by simply defining what type of thinking is taking place between the supervisor and the employee.

In 1991, deBono completed the series on thinking by proposing the notion of the system of thinking called **Six Action Shoes.** He used these to describe how certain thinking patterns resulted in actions which the individual can and does invoke as a result of the cerebral work.

What are the action shoes?

1. NAVY SHOES: Navy action mode is for routine behavior.
2. GREY SNEAKERS: Grey sneaker action mode is for information and thinking about it.
3. BROWN BROGUES: Brown brogue action mode is for emphasizing pragmatism and practicality. It is a matter of doing what can be done.
4. ORANGE BOOTS: Orange gumboot action mode has to do with emergencies, crises, and dangerous situations. When situations are unstable, unpredictable, and likely to get worse, urgent action is required.
5. PINK SLIPPERS: Pink slipper action mode is concerned with human caring, with sympathy, compassion, and help.
6. PURPLE BOOTS: Purple riding boot action mode reflects authority and playing an official role.

Supervisors must possess a willing-to-learn approach to making sound managerial decisions. Using strategies such as these suggested by deBono can make the learning process much easier for the supervisor who wants to improve his or her ability to make effective decisions and solve problems. The scope of this paper does not permit a more in-depth discussion of deBono's CoRT Thinking System. However, from what was described above, the supervisor who utilizes these thinking techniques in problem solving will certainly be much better prepared to effectively discharge this aspect of his or her duties.

Avoiding decisions is not uncommon for people and especially for supervisors who do not want to make a decision because they do not want to face the consequences. If a supervisor finds him or herself in this situation, an effective way to overcome this condition is to ask the following questions to determine if any of these are the reasons for postponing it:

1. You decide there aren't enough facts to make the decision. Therefore, you decide to postpone making it until you get **all** the information.
2. You decide that it is not important enough to bother with--then you assign it to a subordinate to make.
3. You assign the problem to a committee to decide. This will probably delay the decision indefinitely.
4. You undertake research on the topic to find out how such a problem was previously solved. This could cause the decision to be put off for months.
5. You postpone making the decision because of "illness" or a "more pressing problem."
6. You decide that you don't have the authority to make the decision and that it should be made by someone else.
7. You decide to wait until next week when you will have more time to devote to giving the matter your undivided attention. Next week, of course, seldom comes (George, 1970, p. 87).

Supervisors ducking the decision making process will eventually doom themselves to failure. There is no way to supervise effectively and not make decisions that result in some consequence.

Robbins (1985) maintained that "every action produces some outcome. There is no such thing as failure. If an action does not produce the outcome you want, analyze what you got from your initial action, modify your behavior, and produce some new action. Continue doing this until you produce the outcome you want. See, there is not such thing as failure. There is only a failure to act."

The rule to avoid making decisions is to understand yourself and postpone making decisions only for good sound reasons. Putting a decision into effect, watching it produce the results, and seeing the results move the organization forward toward its goal is the paramount reason for the supervisor to act.

Some practical tips on making sound decisions are:
1. Decide whether the decision is a big or small one. If it is a big problem, give it full treatment. Weigh all aspects of it carefully. Big problems demand all the time, attention, and skill that the supervisor can give it. Little problems don't deserve the trappings of a "summit conference." Debating on whether or not to stop for a coffee break at 10 or 10:15 am is one way to stifle any forward progress.
2. Don't make snap decisions. Take time to get the facts and then analyze them carefully.
3. Rely on established company policy and practices where possible. If company policy is to suspend an employee found drinking on the job, this is the answer if you face such a problem.
4. Seek the help of others when you are in doubt. Ask other people what they think, especially people who are well informed and whose judgement you trust.
5. Avoid crisis decisions. Most of the time, decisions do not need to be made spontaneously. Ask yourself when the decision has to be made. Then utilize the time available to make the best decisions. If there is a crisis, remember that you are the "boss" and your employees are looking to you for a decision.
6. If a decision has to be made, make it. Don't put off making a needed decision. This will only make work pile up even higher.

7.   Don't brood over a decision once action has been taken. Evaluation, yes; brooding, no. Poor decisions are made by many people every day, from the President of the United States on down. As consolation, we seldom make a decision that is really wrong. In most cases, we make decisions that are effective or ineffective. Once you've put a decision into effect, worrying about it won't make it any better or worse. Learn from it. Produce new action. Then learn from it. Learn from it. Produce new action. This is the way to effectively make decisions that in the end, produce the results that you want and solve the problems (George, 1979, p. 91).

Using the deBono thinking methods, the strategies suggested by George, and then making decisions that are based upon the most realistic appraisal of what the situation is and demands can save the supervisor many agonizing moments in dispatching his or her duties. What makes supervision exciting is not the fact that problems exist and must be solved causing decisions to be made, but once they are, not just the supervisor, the employees, but the entire organization benefits from the energy expended.

7. SUPERVISORS IN ACTION

The **Golden Rule of Supervision** is: Any order that cannot be understood cannot be executed.

Communicating to other people what they are to do is the way any supervisor gets things done. In this way, a supervisor's decisions and ideas implemented. How the supervisor tells them what to do will determine how well the job will be done and whether or not the supervisor will succeed or fail in his or her endeavors.

George (1979) described six simple rules the effective supervisor needs to follow to be effective in providing direction for employees. They are:

1.   **Create the right climate.** Directions need to be given in a climate and spirit of help and cooperation. Commands and brusque orders are the mark of an immature supervisor and seldom achieve more than a grudging compliance. Creating this type of climate does not happen overnight. Where employees willingly and enthusiastically accept a directive, the supervisor can be sure that a climate of helpful cooperation exists.

2.   **Make the direction reasonable.** A good direction is a reasonable one. A direction that is reasonable for one employee may not be for another one. Remember that individual differences exist within all work environments.

3.   **Make the direction understandable.** Any order that cannot be understood cannot be executed. Be sure then that the order is understood by the employee. How directions are communicated depends on the employee and the situation. Some employees need more direction; some need very little. Whatever the situation, be sure the employee understands your point of view and knows exactly what you want done.

4.   **Choose the right words.** When giving a direction, use the right words and say them in such a way that the employee enthusiastically accepts the direction. At times a direct command is needed. On most occasions, it is better to request that someone do something rather than demand it.

5.   **Explain the "Why" of the Direction.** If there is the slightest chance the employee will not understand why something needs to be done, be sure to tell him or her. If he or she understands why he or she was given the direction, he or she is more likely to pitch in and get the work accomplished with dispatch.

6.   **Be prepared for problems.** No matter how carefully you go through the previous steps in giving directions, you are bound to have problems. This is just part of the job. Explain to the employee what is needed. Listen to his or her concerns. Follow up on directions given. Process the results with the employee. Acknowledge his or her successfully completing what was directed of him or her (George, 1979, p. 113-115).

What if the employee refuses to follow a direction even after being requested to do so? This is not an uncommon occurrence. When there are problems, patience is necessary. Remember that the goal is to get the job done. It is then the responsibility of the supervisor to ask:

1.   Did he understand the direction?

2.   Is he willfully refusing or is there some reason why he did not do what was asked of him that is not obvious?

3.   If is not obvious, ask him, "Is there something here that I need to know about that you aren't telling me?"

4.   Ask, "Is there something that I did or said that is getting in the way of your doing what I asked you to do?"

Should supervisors give answers to their employees when they ask for solutions to problems? In general, no. To do so is poor supervision. Solving a problem for an employee disempowers him or her and it does not place him or her in a place to make a decision on his or her own the next time a similar problem is encountered. What effective supervisors do in this type of situation is engage the employee in creative problem solving. Assisting the employee in discovering the answer for him or herself is much more productive and empowers the employee to continue to problem solve on his or her own in the future.

Giving the employee the answer is much simpler and more time efficient. However, one of the most important functions of supervision is to train the employee to be better at all aspects of his or her job related responsibilities and problem solving is one of the most important activities of any employee's functions. The better each individual employee is at problem solving the less time the supervisor will spend solving problems for others. Time management is the key issue. Time spent initially problem solving with an employee will pay great dividends later on.

This process is like the answer the little boy gave to a teacher when she asked him if he bought a cart for $6.92 and sold it for $8.24, whether he would win or lose on the deal. He thought about it for a moment and then said, he would win on the dollars but lose on the cents. In helping an employee solve his own problems you may lose on the cents (the short run), but you will win on the dollars (the long run).

What are the signals that a supervisor is not doing an effective job? There is no one signal that clearly indicates that a supervisor is doing an ineffective job. However, several factors combined might tell him or her that something is not working. The following checklist (George, 1979) can be used by any supervisor to measure his or her supervisory performance. If two or more of these items apply to the supervisor, it may signal that something may be amiss.

The Supervisory Problems Check List is on the next page.

SUPERVISORY PROBLEMS CHECK LIST

1. Do you get complaints from your employees about the quality and delivery of your work?
2. Are costs increasing in your department that you can't justify?
3. Is production output per employee decreasing?
4. Have you had increases in the number of complaints or grievances within the past year?
5. Have you had to reprimand several of your employees during the past year for conflicts, hostility, and unjustified actions?
6. Do you have to watch your employees more closely than you used to because they no longer are self starters?
7. Is there indication of apathy and disinterest among your employees about their jobs and the company?
8. During meetings, do you find that attendance is poor and little interest shown in the topic being discussed?
9. Do your employees misunderstand your instructions and not do what you tell them to do?
10. Are there increased absences and turnover?

Eventually, every employee problem affects work. In such instances, an understanding and cooperative supervisor who recognizes these problems can do much to help his or her employees get over this difficult time.

Supervisory counseling is nothing more than talking in private with an employee. Listening carefully to what the employee has to say. Don't argue and don't criticize him. Try to understand what he or she is trying to say. Like an iceberg, only 10% of an employee's feelings are on the surface. The other 90% are below the surface. A conscientious supervisor attempts to discover these hidden feelings through an intimate talk with his or her employee.

The session may provide the employee with sound advice or with hope and reassurance. It may help him or her to clarify his or her own thinking. These sessions may assist the employee in bridging the gap between supervisor and employee. In such sessions, the supervisor's role is to serve as a fact finder and listening post.

Generally, the most difficult problems to identify and correct are personal problems. Whatever they are, they certainly will affect the employee's work performance. Personal problems may be interrelated with all sorts of other problems. Even though the supervisor may not like it, counseling troubled employees is a necessary part of being effective. Remember, that problem employees can do more harm than good if they are not helped.

To describe all the nuances of the supervisor's role when he or she is actively dispatching supervisory duties would take thousands of volumes of text and is beyond the scope of this paper. Suffice it to say, the supervisor who hopes to be not only an effective supervisor but a leader as well, needs to master these suggested skills and many more not listed here. Reading, attending supervisory training, watching other effective supervisors work and role modeling their actions, practicing counseling techniques, learning to become an active listener, are all actions which will enhance the effectiveness of any supervisor.

8. THE SUPERVISOR AS MOTIVATOR

Supervisors need to motivate their employees to work--to make them want to do their jobs. The question is how does the supervisor actually motivate others to perform up their individual potential?

Employees possess certain needs and wants that they bring to work with them. These are called **motives**. They are the things which make employees do the things they do. Everything an employee does is to satisfy a motive. If an employee fails to do something, it generally is because he or she does not see any personal advantage in doing it. It does not satisfy some motive.

What kinds of **motives** do employees possess? Let's examine this further.

Maslow (1954) described the basic needs of human beings as follows:

1. ***Basic Physical Needs***. The basic necessities of life are food, shelter, clothing, rest, reproduction, and the other physical needs that are instinctive in all of us so that we might survive.

2. ***Safety Needs***. Once our basic physical needs are somewhat satisfied, our thoughts turn to the need to protect ourselves from danger, to be secure. We want freedom from worry about our future welfare, and normally this means job security to most of us. We want to feel that our jobs are secure and that we will have an income until we retire.

3. ***Social Needs***. All of us want to feel that we are "in"--that we are a member of or belong to a certain group. This is the social need. It is to belong to a part of a group, and to be accepted and respected by other members of the group is a strong urge in all of us.

4.   ***Esteem Needs***. Closely related to the social need is the need for self-respect, or the need to be recognized for who we are and what makes us unique. All of us feel this need when we want recognition, status, achievement, or a sense of accomplishment. It is basically respect for self. The individual feels that what he is doing what he was put there to do. Esteem needs are very powerful needs because they relate to feelings of worth and importance.

5.   ***Self-Actualization Needs***. Self-actualization needs are what psychologists call the highest order of needs. After the first four needs have been somewhat satisfied, then we experience the need for self-actualization. We want to feel that we have accomplished things to best of our abilities--our potentialities. When we have met this need, we say to ourselves that we have become all that we are capable of becoming. When we have met this need, we have been fully creative and are occupied in performing to the limits of our capacities. Not many of us turn to this need because we are so busy trying to satisfy social and esteem needs (Chapter 5).

Every person is different. The major influence is individual biological makeup. Age, sex, weight, height, race, physique are factors that bear on our personalities. Childhood plays a large part in determining our later adjustment and personality. Such factors as feeding patterns, environmental conditions, family units, and training patterns are things which affect personality and adjustment. Finally, the broad culture in which we grow up profoundly influences the individual. The American culture stresses freedom of choice, competition, equal opportunity, and rewards for accomplishment. Individuals growing up in America have a strong regard for a good day's work, and a belief that if they work hard enough, they can live "The American Dream."

All people are a product of their inherited physical makeup, early childhood, and culture. These factors make us who we are, and supervisors need to recognize this.

The supervisor's job is to get others to do things because they want to do them. The successful supervisor is one who provides his or her employees with the opportunity to satisfy their own needs. They will work because they see that by doing so they will satisfy their individual needs. Before a supervisor can provide this opportunity to employees, he or she must first be aware of the types of things that motivate his or her employees.

Matching jobs and individual needs is one way to satisfy employees' needs. If an employee is placed in a position which is challenging and satisfies his or her needs, motivation will not be a problem. This may mean reworking jobs to make them more complex, more challenging, and hopefully, more satisfying to the employee. Matching employee needs with jobs is a very difficult process. Once the supervisor understands what an employee's basic needs are, he or she can be more sensitive to these needs and try to match the employee with jobs that offer him or her the opportunity to satisfy individual needs.

Menninger and Levinson (1956) surveyed thousands of employees in many different industries. In the survey, supervisors were asked to rank ten job factors in the same way they thought their employees would. Then the employees were asked to rank these same ten factors in order of their importance to them. The results show that many supervisors did not understand what workers wanted out of their jobs. See Figure 1 on the next page.

SUPERVISOR-EMPLOYEE MOTIVATION SURVEY

Employee Ranking	Item Being Rated	Supervisor Ranking
1	Appreciation of work well done	8
2	Feeling of being "in on things"	10
3	Help on personal problems	9
4	Job security	2
5	Good wages	1
6	Interesting work	5
7	Promotion and growth in company	3
8	Personal loyalty to employees	6
9	Good working conditions	4
10	Tactful disciplining	7

(p. 12)

This research does not prove that money, good working conditions, and loyalty to employees are unimportant. These factors are extremely important and companies need to continually strive to be competitive in these areas. All ten factors are important needs to all employees. Most employees expect a company to provide good working conditions, fair pay, opportunity for growth, and interesting work. Most companies attempt to provide these. Lower ranked needs are very important and if they are not satisfied, they will cause employees to be less motivated to achieve higher needs. What is important for the supervisor to distill from the research is that the needs which are most important to most employees are social and esteem needs. The effective supervisor then, should pay close attention to these areas.

George (1979) encouraged supervisors to use the following strategies in meeting the social and esteem needs of their employees:
1. Treat employees as individuals.
2. Be sincere with praise.
3. Promote participation.
4. Make the work interesting.
5. Promote cooperation and teamwork.
6. Provide growth opportunities (p. 136).

There is no formula for motivating employees. George (1979) wrote that the best approach for getting employees to work along with him or her is to remember the following:
1. Communicate with your employees and praise them.
2. Consult with your employees about their work.
3. Encourage your employees to participate in setting goals on the job.
4. Counsel your employees about teamwork, opportunity, and so on.

What are the characteristics of the supervisor who most successfully motivates his or her employees? He or she is not the bull-of-the-woods tough guy or gal, or the one who uses fear. The supervisor who motivates best is not the one who plays his or her cards "close to his chest" and makes all the decisions him or herself.

George (1979) concluded that the supervisor who motivates his or her employees best is one who:

1. Establishes realistic goals for him or herself and others--goals that are worthwhile, challenging, and attainable.

2. Makes decisions after relevant participation by his or her subordinates. He seeks and is seriously interested in their thoughts and ideas.

3. Seeks and gives feedback to his or her employees about how they are doing, the progress they are making, and the problems that are coming up. Because of his or her open communication and feedback, his employees are motivated to perform well. They openly evaluate their progress, and they do not hesitate to seek changes when they think they are needed.

4. Resolves conflicts with good judgment, understanding, and openness. The supervisor focuses on solving the conflict rather than placing blame. He or she attempts to understand the problem and find the best solution.

5. Always communicates to his or her employees, explaining what is being done and why it is being done. He talks honestly and openly about how he or she feels about things. This process of open and continuous communication lets the employees know what is going on inside him or her.

6. Always listens to what his or her employees tell him, tries to understand what they are saying, and makes good comments about their ideas. He or she doesn't hesitate to question them and ask them, "How about explaining that again to me?" Being listened to makes the employee feel important and also makes him or her more willing to listen to what the boss says.

7. Is genuinely interested in his or her employees as individuals. He is interested in their growth and future progress.

8. Is open and sincere in his praise, reprimands in private, and praises in public.

9. Controls his or her temper. When angry, the supervisor doesn't brood. He or she approaches the employee and directly and expresses his or her feelings honestly. This can encourage dialogue between the supervisor and employee and a major crisis can be disposed of as a minor problem.

10. Is open-minded, always willing to listen to new ideas, even those that are different from his or her own. He or she doesn't mind criticism and readily admits to his or her mistakes. He or she is the type of person the employee would like to have as a personal friend.

11. Uses reprimands only when necessary and even then delivers them in private. He or she uses them to educate and correct and not to punish an employee.

12. Makes jobs as interesting and desirable as possible.

13. Is not afraid to delegate and willingly gives credit to his or her employees for a job well-done.

14. Doesn't try to get work out of his or her employees by threatening them.

15. Is not afraid to admit he or she is wrong and his or her employees are right.

16. Actively seeks the opportunity to promote his or her employees--even if it means losing them.

17. Tries to run an orderly department, bringing system to an otherwise confused situation.

18. Is big enough not to compete with his or her employees for credit. He or she lets employees bask in the spotlight for a job well done.

19. Is not condescending.

20. Is not a know-it-all (pp. 138-139).

Finally, the supervisor who motivates best is the Theory Y supervisor (McGregor, 1960). This supervisor supports the employees meeting their higher-level needs. His or her approach is to supervise in such a way that social and esteem needs can be met so that the employees can feel self-actualized.

9. SUPERVISORS AND EMPLOYEE EVALUATIONS

As a supervisory tool, employee evaluations serve to quantitatively measure an employee's work performance. As a motivational tool, employee evaluations can serve to affirm an individual employee's satisfactory, above average, or exceptional performance. The problem with most Performance Evaluations (PE) is that they are not done on time, are not objective, and are not done, in most organizations, frequently enough to effectively motivate individual employees.

A PE consists of a systematic appraisal of the employee's performance and of his or her potential for development and training. It is usually done by the employee's immediate supervisor and is then reviewed by the supervisor's superior. Reviewing the PE with the employee, pointing out strengths and indicating areas needing improvement, is essential if the employee is to improve his or her work performance.

Many methods are used including the Rating-Scale Method, Comparison Method, and the Essay Method. All have their advantages and disadvantages. No matter how much care the supervisor gives to evaluating his or her employees, the results frequently reflect the supervisor's biases and weaknesses.

The **"halo effect"** occurs when a supervisor lets the rating he or she gives an employee in one area affect the rating he or she gives in another area. The supervisor may say the employee is average in his job skill and then have a tendency to rate everything else about the employee as average.

Some supervisors tend to be **too lenient or too strict**. Others are tough. It's difficult to decide on which of two employees to promote when each of them has been rated by different supervisors-- one tough and one lenient in his or her appraisal.

Some supervisors don't know their employees well enough, so they don't go out on the limb and say anyone is either superior or poor. Therefore, they rank everyone as **average**. Supervisors who do this believe they don't hurt anyone this way, but they are not helping the deserving ones either.

Personal biases can cause problems. A supervisor sometimes unconsciously rates an employee according to whether or not he or she personally likes the employee.

The **end use** of appraisals also materially affects the way supervisors rate average employees. If the supervisor knows the appraisals are to be used for wage increases, the ratings will tend to be higher than normal so that the employee will get a pay increase. If they are to be used to determine whether or not the employee needs training in an area, they are apt to be a little on the low side.

The thrust of the PE interview is for the supervisor to review the progress the employee made since his or her last evaluation. Areas in which the employee made significant improvement need to be pointed out. In areas where progress has not been shown, the supervisor should make constructive suggestions for improvement. An interview is almost always doomed to failure when the supervisor saves up a list of shortcomings and unloads them on the employee during the interview. The PE interview should give the employee an opportunity to discuss his or her job problems and aspirations with his or her supervisor, as well as give the supervisor the opportunity to assist the employee become a better worker. Finally, the supervisor needs to make sure that the employee clearly understands the ratings and there are no unanswered questions. Given the proper encouragement, most employees will emerge from an PE interview with renewed vigor and determination to do a better job.

George (1979) listed several advantages that can be gained from using an employee evaluation program:

1. You have a permanent written record of the relative strengths and weaknesses of your employees, which can be used for salary changes, promotions, transfers, demotions, etc.

2. It forces you to evaluate an employee's performance and potential--forces you as a supervisor to analyze the strengths and weaknesses of each of his or her employees. Thus, you know them better, thereby putting you in a position to do a better job as a supervisor.
3. In case of contention over promotion, pay, and the like, you have a sound basis for your decision.
4. Once an employee comes to understand some of his weaknesses, he will be stimulated to set goals to improve him or herself.
5. Areas in which training is needed become more obvious, and training courses can be set up.
6. An individual employee's talents are more apt to be recognized and used where they are most needed in the organization.
7. The evaluation serves to help eliminate employees being poorly placed or misplaced (p. 198).

Finally, George (1979) offered the following tips on how to effectively use PE's in organizations:
1. Never let employees evaluate or rate each other. This is management's responsibility and should be done by a member of the supervisory staff.
2. Never discuss one employee's rating with another employee.
3. Evaluate the employee's performance at least once a year. Twice a year is better. If you wait too long, you forget. If you rate too often, you see day-to-day occurrences instead of the overall picture.
4. Measure an employee's skill against what the job description reads, not what you think he or she can do. This makes the evaluation more accurate.
5. Take plenty of time for the evaluation interview. Don't let the phone ring during it, or permit other employees come in and interrupt.
6. Always include discussion of goals and mutually agreed upon improvement programs for the next appraisal period.

7. Don't terminate an interview until you have cleared up all misunderstandings about the present rating, future goals, and what the employee expects.

8. Be honest and candid in your appraisal. If an employee's work has been poor, say so. Then assist him or her in seeing where and how it can be improved.

9. Soften your criticism by saying something positive. Without a balanced delivery, the employee may become defensive and effectively tune out anything constructive you might say later.

10. Follow up interviews by subsequently checking with your employees on how they are performing, the progress they are making, and what their problems are. This demonstrates interest on your part and can serve as a stimulus for the employees to strive for improvement (p. 199).

It is impossible for a supervisor to accurately evaluate any employee unless he or she actually watches the employee perform his or her job. Too often, supervisors are busy and assume they can see or hear what an employee is doing, and yet do not. Observing an employee on the job once or twice during an evaluation period is not enough. If PE's are only done once a year, then a supervisor needs to observe his or her employees in action at least once a month at a minimum to be able to objectively evaluate his or her employee. The surest way to create defensiveness in an employee is to evaluate him or her when there has been no direct observation on the supervisor's part at any time during the evaluation period. Being able to reference observations with the evaluation can and will eliminate defensiveness.

Every effort needs to be made by the supervisor to base every evaluation on the context of the employee's overall job and on the employee's total job performance. Basing a rating on only one aspect of an employee's performance or on the way he or she performed on a particular job would not be fair. Instead, the appraisal needs to be based on the total record of what the employee has done, how well he or she has performed, his or her total reliability, resourcefulness, and so on. Evaluations are not perfect, but with some thought and work on the supervisor's part, they can be fairly objective and can serve useful ends in rewarding and ultimately, motivating employees.

10. ASSERTIVE SUPERVISION

The terms nonassertive, aggressive, and assertive can be used both positively and negatively. Nonassertive often refers to both a polite, deferential style of interaction and a wishy-washy approach. The term aggressive refers to described a forceful, energetic, approach to the world and to describe someone who acts in ways that infringe upon others. Assertive is used in both positive and negative ways. For some, assertive is associated with clear, confident communication. For others, it represents a selfish, egocentric approach to life that undermines working together to common goals.

A supervisor acting non-assertively does not say what he or she wants or feels, speaks indirectly or apologetically, says something about a problem to the wrong problem to the wrong person, waits too long to confront a problem, gives up too easily, and compromises without making his or her needs clear. He or she tends to use words, voice characteristics, and body language that appear pleading and wishy-washy and tend to be discounted or elicit argument from others.

The supervisor acting aggressively tends to blame and make judgmental criticisms, attribute negative intentions to others, act with too much power and too quickly, and refuse to listen or negotiate and compromise. The words he or she chooses and his voice characteristics and body language tend to put others on the defensive and make them feel threatened or cornered.

Finally, the assertive supervisor makes clear, direct, non-apologetic statements about his or her expectations and feelings, criticizes in a descriptive rather than a judgmental way, persists following through on issues even if he meets resistance, listens to others' views respectfully, and negotiates and compromises. He or she does all of these things using words, voice characteristics, and body language that will be taken seriously without humiliating others.

Many stereotypes about assertiveness exist. Some of these images come from popular literature, some from observing or talking to people who have attended assertive training workshops and some from the assertive literature itself (Smith, 1975). To destroy stereotypical notions regarding assertiveness, consider the following conditions under which it is the most productive supervisory style.

1.   Assertiveness is not a "do your own thing" philosophy. Although assertiveness techniques can be used to pursue personal instead of organizational goals, assertiveness here is used in the service of effectively carrying out the supervisor's obligations to the organization. In the assertiveness model being described, insisting on "doing your own thing" and ignoring organizational priorities and the rights and needs of others is aggressive and not assertive.

2.   Asserting yourself doesn't guarantee you will always get what you want. Many people believe that assertiveness implies getting their own way regardless of others' needs and priorities. This often leads to unpleasant social interactions. It is also unrealistic. There are many personal and organizational constraints on everyone. Assertion often requires imaginatively looking for alternative ways to solve a problem when personal or organizational constraints make a particular change impossible. An assertive supervisor would look for ways to streamline time-consuming paperwork when a tight budget makes assertion to get more staff impractical, rather than helplessly saying, "Oh, isn't this awful? Someone should do something." Assertiveness does not require that a supervisor continue to "beat her head against a brick wall." Continuing to push for change when constraints are made clear can create a great deal of frustration and therefore damage the supervisor's effectiveness on issues where change is possible.

3.	Assertiveness is not an invitation to be rude, obnoxious, and unpleasant. There is no incompatibility between assertiveness and courtesy. Assertiveness requires courteous, respectful treatment of others. It is the embodiment of the "Golden Rule." It implies that you should respect and value others and respect and value yourself. It is entirely possible to be powerful and firm and to be polite and respectful at the same time. Finally, assertiveness emphasizes a respectful firmness.

4.	You don't have to be assertive all the time. It is unlikely that anyone can be assertive all of the time. People vary in their strengths and weaknesses in their ability to be assertive. Assertiveness does not pretend to create a rigid new set of rules for all behavior in all situations. Aggressive and nonassertive approaches may be the most effective responses in certain circumstances. Sometimes it may not be worth the risk to be assertive. Some employees, for instance, will respond to another style (Drury, 1984).

In the context of Assertive Supervision, the following underlying assumptions are made regarding human nature and how people want and need to be treated. They dovetail nicely with principles presented earlier in the section on motivating employees.

1.	People want to do a good job (McGregor, 1960).

2.	People have a powerful need to save face (Maslow, 1954).

3.	Failing to tell someone about a problem is not doing him a favor (Alberti & Emmons, 1975).

4.	No one can force anyone else to change (Bower & Bower, 1975).

5.	Assertiveness will not always work right away (Jubowski & Lange, 1978).

Supervisory style is a powerful influence on building involved teamwork. Style consists of what action a supervisor takes and how quickly. Employees respond differently to nonassertive, aggressive, and assertive styles. Though all three styles are sometimes necessary, Drury (1984) maintained that an overall assertive approach is the best one for building teamwork within an organization.

Changing behavior is difficult, and if a supervisor's style is not assertive but predominately, one of the other two, change can be painful. New assertive behaviors may feel awkward for a time. Change takes time, and the supervisor practicing assertiveness is encouraged to do so in simple situations first and not in complex ones.

According to Drury (1984) nonassertive supervisors follow certain patterns of behavior. These affect their performance and the performance of their employees and co-workers. What are these characteristics?

1. **No expression of expectations and feelings.**
   Question: Do you find yourself holding back your views on issues, particularly when you sense that the other person might disagree or be upset by your views?

2. **Views stated indirectly and apologetically.**
   Question: In an effort to be tactful, do you disguise your opinions so well that others have to guess what you really mean?

3. **Complaints often made to the wrong person.**
   Question: Do you find that you often complain about situations to someone who can't do anything to change the situation?

4. **Problems are not confronted soon enough.**
   Question: Do you often put off raising issues you know you should confront?

5. **No persistence.**
   Question: Do you find that you often end up giving in when you start out being assertive?
6. **Unclear negotiation and compromise.**
   Question: Do you find yourself not stating what you want when you are negotiating or compromising?

On the following page is a self-test to measure your understanding of the nonassertive supervisory style.

NONASSERTIVE SUPERVISORY SELF-TEST

Directions: Pick the nonassertive response in the following situations and specify what cues you used.

1. Cora has an employee who comes to her several times an hour for help on problems she could solve herself.
   a. Cora complains to her supervisor almost daily about the worker.
   b. Cora tells the employee she needs to attempt to solve problems herself before asking for help.

2. Don is convinced that the new reporting procedure is slowing productivity and has some data to prove it.
   a. He schedules a meeting with his supervisor to discuss the data and talk about possible ways to modify the procedure.
   b. He hopes management will see and correct the obvious problem.

3. Laura needs her manager's backing when she confronts an employee.
   a. She has a conversation with her supervisor about problem employees in general and the need for management support.
   b. She has a conversation with the supervisor in which she describes the situation with that employee and asks whether the supervisor will support her in reprimanding that employee.

4. Danielle has been taking on extra work from another unit.
   a. She will say something as soon as she begins to feel this is a problem.
   b. She lets the situation go until she is fuming about the unfair and unreasonable demands of the other departments and then has an angry confrontation.

Answers are on the next page.

Answers to Self-Test

1.   a is the nonassertive response because she complains to the wrong person. b is assertive because she makes her comments to the person involved.

2.   b is the nonassertive response because he does not express his expectations and feelings but just waits for the situation to change. a is assertive because he takes an active role.

3.   a is the nonassertive response because she is too direct in expressing what she wants. b is assertive because she expresses her feelings when the problem begins.

4.   b is the nonassertive response because she waits too long to confront the problem. a is assertive because she expresses her feelings when the problem begins.

Certain kinds of language present cues to reveal the nonassertive supervisory style. One way that a supervisor can learn to identify his or her style is to listen to the words used in interactions with employees.

Minimizing words. Phrases and words like kind of, a little, sort of, maybe, and perhaps, inadvertently tell others that particular communications are not to be taken seriously. One way that someone appears nonassertive and dilutes his impact on others is by using minimizing words. People are less likely to pay attention to statements that are delivered in a minimized way (Eisen, 1984).

Apologetic statements. Nonassertive responses are often preceded or followed by phrases that reduce their impact. Sentences like "I know that this will be a bother and you probably won't want to do it, but could you possibly help me with this project?" and "I'd really like some help with this project if you don't mind too much and can fit it into your schedule with no hassle" are examples of this (Smith, 1975).

Statements made about people in general instead of to a specific person. Nonassertive supervisors will sometimes confront a problem with a particular employee by announcing in a meeting that "Some people around here have been taking too long a lunch hour lately." The guilty person is often insensitive to the statement being made. A motivated, cooperative employee might very well take the hint, examine his performance, and makes the necessary changes without any more specific intervention from the supervisor. The less motivated, less self-aware employee could easily fail to see the message relevant to him (Eisen, 1985).

General instead of specific behavioral descriptions. Employees need to know exactly what they are doing to create a problem if they are to be able to change. One common nonassertive word choice is to use general, inclusive descriptions of problems rather than pinpointing specific performance problems. Comments like "Your performance could be better" or "Your performance is inadequate" or "You should work harder" might serve as effective introductions to a clearer, more specific description of the problem. If a supervisor tells an employee to "work harder," he may mean that he wants the employee to take shorter lunch hours, not to make personal phone calls, to increase the pace of his work, not to make so many trips to the water cooler, or any number of other specific behaviors (Eisen, 1985).

Statements disguised as questions. Another common nonassertive word choice is to ask a question that is really a disguised request or statement of opinion. "You wouldn't want to use that procedure with this problem, would you?" or "Don't you think that Mr. Jones is being unfair?" are questions that permit the questioner to express a point of view without having to take responsibility for it. There are many people who respond to this type of rhetorical questioning by treating it as a pure question (Eisen, 1985).

The impact of an interaction is determined not only by the words used, but also by the voice characteristics and by body language. Nonverbal cues are often far more important determinants of other's reaction than verbal cues (Henley, 1977). Becoming aware of nonverbal cues requires careful observation of self and others.

Some of these are:
1.   Pleading or questioning voice tone.
2.   Lack of eye contact.
3.   Hesitation.
4.   Slumping downtrodden posture.
5.   Words and nonverbal messages that don't match.

Non-assertiveness does cause problems for the supervisor. Some of these problems are:
1.   Physical tension.
2.   An "unfinished" feeling.
3.   Resentment.
4.   Uncertainty.
5.   Negative feelings.
6.   Lack of respect.
7.   Attack and manipulation.

When is the nonassertive supervisory style the best? Here are some situations.
1.   When the risks of assertiveness are too great.
2.   When it is simply not worth the trouble to be assertive.
3.   When it is not the appropriate time to be assertive.

There are four major inhibitions to assertiveness. These are:
1.   Guilt.
2.   Fear and anxiety.
3.   Doubt.
4.   Nice-guy Image.

Each of the four above inhibitions can seriously affect the supervisor's ability to be assertive. When these are present, it is difficult for the nonassertive supervisor to change his or her style even though it may be extremely necessary.

The following behavior patterns, Drury (1985) wrote, characterize an **Aggressive supervisory style**. All these patterns have in common the tendency to make people defensive.

1. **Critical expression of expectations and feelings.** Aggressive people express their expectations and feeling by attacking the other person. The most common effect of this kind of management style is to put the other person on the defensive. People tend to stop listening when they feel they are being attacked and thus don't hear the part of the message that may be constructive.

   Question: Are you critical of others when you express your expectations and feelings?

2. **Blaming and judgmental criticisms.** When there is a problem, the aggressive supervisor usually will attack the other person rather than describe the situation and discuss strategies for solving the problem. The emphasis is on discovering who is to blame for the problem instead of working together to solve the problem. The aggressive supervisor believes that making an employee accept blame for problems and see his or her problems and see her personality faults is often thought of as a way to motivate the person to change.

   Question: Do you find yourself that you often make assumptions about what particular employee actions mean?

3. **"Muscle level" too high.** Muscle level refers to the strength or leverage of someone's interactions with others. There are four levels of muscle (Butler, 1976).

Muscle Level I is a polite request: "I'd like you to let us know when you can't come to a steering committee meeting."

Muscle Level II is a request that is stronger in word choice, voice characteristics, and body language. "When you don't let us know that you're going to miss a meeting, we sometimes end up meeting without a quorum, which is useless. I need to know when you can't make a meeting."

Muscle Level III is a statement of the consequences if the behavior doesn't change: "If you can't let us know when you'll miss a meeting we will have to ask you to resign from the committee."

Muscle Level IV is the application of the consequences stated in Level III: "Since you have not been keeping us informed about your attendance, I will have to ask you to leave the committee."

> Question: Do you find that sometimes you use Muscle Level III responses without using Levels I and II first? If so, what happens?

4. **Problems acted on too quickly.** While the nonassertive person waits too long to act, the aggressive person often "shoots from the hip" - acts too quickly without finding out all of the facts. Aggressive people tend to draw very quick conclusions, when coupled with a tendency not to listen carefully to others, can lead to impulsive action. Aggressive action can interfere with systematic problem solving.

> Question: Do you find yourself acting on issues quickly without considering all aspects of the situation and potential solutions?

5. **Unwillingness to listen.** If others' ideas are basically seen as irrelevant or wrong, there is no particular reason to listen to them. The aggressive person is much more likely to interrupt someone to finish what he or she wants to say than to stop and listen to the other person. In a crisis, aggressive people are much more likely to say what they think about the problem over and over than to try to find out how someone else sees the problem. The disadvantage of this is that the aggressive person misses a great deal of useful information by not listening.

   Question: Do the people who work with you seem to feel free to talk to you about problems?

6. **Refusal to negotiate and compromise.** The aggressive person wants what he or she wants when he or she wants it. Since aggressive people are generally convinced that they are right and that their priorities are most important, they simply are not interested in negotiation and compromise. They often view other peoples' needs or organizational priorities as attempts to question their authority or sabotage their work.

   Question: Do you find yourself insisting that everything be done your way (pp. 52-54)?

The kinds of words used by a supervisor are often a reflection of the aggressive style. Loaded words like lazy, incompetent, stupid, unmotivated, and worthless are judgmental in themselves and often provoke a negative reaction. A "you" statement is **you** followed by a loaded word. Even **you** followed by a description of the same behavior tends to provoke more defensiveness than a description of the same behavior done without a verbal finger pointing "you" statement. Another way to put a person on the defensive is to tell him that he "never" does his work on time or the he is "always" late. It is rarely true that a person never does what he is supposed to do. When a supervisor uses "always" or "never" statements, employees will tend to defensively point out the exceptions. Another aggressive approach is to ask a question that really expresses a judgement. The nonassertive person asks a question and hides his feelings. The aggressive person asks a question, but makes his real feelings obvious through word choice, voice tone, and body language.

Assertively phrased sentences can sound quite aggressive if delivered in an aggressive, overbearing tone of voice. Since most people are not aware of their own tone of voice, recognizing this subtle sign of aggressiveness may be difficult. A loud voice volume is one indicator of an aggressive supervisor. Although speaking in a tone of voice that clearly projects is necessary for an assertive style, shouting almost always appears aggressive. Since the aggressive person is not really interested in listening to other people's points of view, she often does not give them an opportunity to finish what they are saying. While the nonassertive person avoids eye contact, the aggressive person may stare at someone without really making eye contact. Staring at someone can certainly be more powerful than not making eye contact at all. This can be intimidating and minimize access to information about the other person's actions. A supervisor can communicate aggressiveness by standing over someone with his or her hands on hips, pointing a finger at someone, or moving so close to someone that personal space is invaded.

Drury (1984) contended that one of the reasons it can be very difficult to alter an aggressive interaction style is that aggressive behavior doesn't create as many painful internal signals that can motivate the supervisor to change. Non-assertiveness is generally accompanied by a great deal of internal tension or a strong sense that somehow something more should be said or done. This is not true of the aggressive person. The aggressive supervisor's most common emotion is anger, or its less controlled form - rage.

The real cue for what aggressive supervision is what it does to others. One way to know if someone is being aggressive is to notice when the other people respond as if they are being attacked. Drury (1984) listed a number of defensive signals that can mean someone feels he is being attacked:

1. Physical withdrawal.
2. Monosyllabic answers or less verbal interaction.
3. Increase in explanations, excuses, or justification.
4. Nonverbal agitation such as fidgeting, breaking eye contact.
5. Anger or frustration, which may emerge as sullenness.
6. Avoidance of contact altogether (p. 62).

There are some situations in which the aggressive supervisory style may be very useful. Using it may be a very effective way to get a person's attention and impress on him or her that the issue being confronted is an important one. Aggressiveness can be used to communicate to a distracted or inattentive employee that the supervisor means business--that he has reached a limit. Becoming aggressive can also be a way to clear the air when a great deal of tension has built up in a relationship. there are times when most people need to just "blow off steam" (Bach & Goldberg, 1974). Some people will escalate conflict in an interaction until they provoke an aggressive response. They see assertiveness as a sign of weakness. With this kind of person, an aggressive approach may be necessary in order for him to recognize that a limit has been set. There are other kinds of power confrontations in which aggressive responses may be necessary in order to intimidate the opponent and thereby enhance personal power and are described in considerable detail in other books (Korda, 1975; Ringer, 1977).

There are many aggressive people who are successful in organizations. They are generally aggressive only when it is not likely to get them in trouble. Aggressiveness is not recommended to supervisors though, because it is a high-risk strategy and the long-term effects on working relationships can be detrimental.

As with the other two, the assertive style is characterized by certain behavior patterns. Drury (1984) maintained that the assertive supervisor can be easily recognized by these effective patterns.

1. **Clear, direct, non-apologetic expression of expectations and feelings.** An assertive supervisor usually states in the first few minutes of an interaction exactly what he or she wants. Statements are specific and are directly addressed to the person for whom they are meant. His or her statements are not buried by apologetic or indirect introductions or followed by rambling comments that blunt their impact. The direct, assertive supervisor takes responsibility for taking care of him or herself in the world. Others do not have to try to take care of him, nor is he dependent on the willingness and ability of others to guess what is needed.

   Question: Do you let others know where you stand on issues?

2. **Descriptive instead of judgmental criticisms.** Assertive criticism describes behavior that is creating problems without attacking the person involved. The purpose of assertive criticism is to solve the problem, not to punish the other person for his or her behavior. The language used is not "loaded" and the process involves mutually exploring what is preventing things from working and generating concrete plans for improvement.

   Question: Do you give your employees feedback when their performance isn't up to standard?

3. **Persistence.** The assertive supervisor will continue to follow through on an issue until it is resolved. He or she looks for other ways to solve a problem when one way is blocked. The Alcoholics Anonymous prayer offers a reasonable motto for assertiveness in business as well:

   God, grant me the courage to change the things that I can change, the serenity to accept the things I cannot change, and the wisdom to know the difference (A.A. International, 1954).

The assertive supervisor takes the stance which involves courage to change what can be changed through persistent, effective action and the serenity to gracefully accept what cannot be changed?

> Question: Are there times when you do not follow through persistently?

4. **Willingness to listen.** An important characteristic of an assertive supervisory style of interaction is to listen to others. In a meeting, the assertive person may disagree with others, but he or she always makes them feel that they have been listened to by him or her. The result of listening effectively is that the supervisor communicates respect for the other persons. The assertive style often takes a little longer initially because it generates a dialogue with the employee. Problems are more likely to be solved because the assertive supervisor finds the source of the problem rather than settling on a quick or arbitrary solution. It is important not only to be able to listen to what others say, but also to be able to communicate to them what is heard. Active listening is a must if the supervisor is to be assertive.

> Question: Can you think of someone in your organization who seems especially good at listening to others?

5. **Negotiation and compromise.** The assertive supervisor is concerned with finding a way that both people in an interaction can win. He or she persists in meeting needs and priorities, but not at the expense of the organization or the people. Judgment, sensitivity, and awareness of self and others are the only guides for effectively balancing personal needs and views with those of other people. The assertive style does not maintain that compromise is always possible. It only says that when possible, compromise and negotiation are likely to lead to more productive teamwork.

Question: Under what circumstances are you willing to negotiate and compromise and how do you make that decision (pp. 79-81)?

Assertive word choices are neither apologetic, angry, nor judgmental, but are neutral and focused on solving problems. Assertive statements command serious attention without arousing defensiveness. They get right to the point. It is not necessary to wade through a lot of language to figure out what the assertive person wants.

The assertive supervisor directs his or her remarks to a specific person and describes specific behaviors. He or she avoids the communication error of bypassing by being precise. The more general the supervisor is when describing behavior, the more danger there is that the other person will misunderstand what she wants.

The assertive supervisor would most likely say such things like "How can we resolve this?" or "Let's work on shortening turnaround time for these new programs." It is essential that the supervisor provide a sense that the supervisor and the employee are working together on a specific problem.

Demands tend to appear much more aggressive than requests. In times of emergency, a demand might be more appropriate, in most cases, employees will be more cooperative when they are asked to do something rather than ordered to do something. Avoiding demands except in emergencies not only elicits more cooperation, it also ensures that when a direction is actually given it is taken seriously. Giving directions in every instance dilutes their effectiveness.

Some of the assertive style's voice characteristics and body language are:
1.   Even, powerful voice tone.
2.   Eye contact.
3.   Erect, relaxed posture.
4.   Words and nonverbal messages match (Drury, 1984, 88).

What are the effects of the assertive style of supervision on the individual? The assertive supervisor possesses a sense of things having a "finished" feeling. There is a sense of relief that accompanies assertive action. He or she does not feel like a victim of circumstances. Employees are more likely to cooperate with an assertive rather than a nonassertive or aggressive supervisor ensuring more teamwork. The assertive style promotes trust because the supervisor is clear about where he or she stands and is willing to listen, negotiate, and compromise. This clear, firm, and fair stand creates a personal commitment within employees to the achievement of organizational priorities and goals.

The basic motto of the assertive person is "I want to find a way for both of us to win. I don't want to ignore my priorities to pay attention to yours" (Drury, 1981, p.92). The most basic support for an assertive approach is to possess a positive self-image, or in Haney's (1986) terminology, and ERSI. The assertive supervisor trusts others. Even though he or she knows some employees will not be motivated to do a good job, he or she tends to assume good intentions (McGregor's Y Theory, 1957) of employees and looks for obstacles to productive work. A feeling of entitlement supports assertiveness, meaning that the supervisor has the right to expect certain kinds of behaviors from his or her employees. The assertive supervisor exhibits objectivity in whatever he or she does. Minor irritations are not made into major catastrophes. He or she bases supervisory behavior on the facts in the situation and not on assumptions about what a particular behavior means.

An assertive supervisory style is necessary if the supervisor hopes to be effective in motivating employees to perform up to their potential in his or her service. This discussion could continue, but for the purposes of this paper, the information provided thus far adequately describes the three styles and how they are interrelated. Each supervisor will eventually choose his or her preference, but given the characteristics of the first two, it is obvious that developing an assertive style will benefit any supervisor in creating an effective team environment which produces the greatest good for the organization, the employees and the supervisor.

11. SUPERVISION IN THE VIRTUAL CORPORATION

As vast amounts of information travel at the speed of light, success in organizations of any kind depends on the survival of the swiftest, the most adaptive supervisors-leaders. Industrial age organizations and traditional management cannot always mobilize resources, supervisors, and employees quickly enough to meet the demands of the fleeting market.

One solution is the establishment of the "Virtual Corporation." But what is a virtual corporation?

Virtual corporations (VC) are strategic business alliances that let firms instantly and dramatically expand their capabilities by pooling talent, expertise, and financial backing to complete a specific project. According to Barnette (1993) "virtual corporations are blurring the traditional boundaries between companies, even creating situations where competitors work side-by-side as temporary partners. They are not only revolutionizing the business world, but also forming the management model of the 21st Century."

Barnette (1993) cites a number of examples. Borland Software and WordPerfect Corporation's co-created a bundled word processor, spreadsheet, database program. Apple Computer joined forces in 1991 with the Sony Corp. to produce the line of PowerBook notebooks, marrying Apple's user-friendly software with Sony's manufacturing and miniaturization expertise. Apple, IBM, and Motorola linked resources to develop an operating system and microprocessor for a new generation of computers.

When problems arise the mobilization of "people power" will be simultaneously swift and unique. Laurie Coots, director of business administration and development at a leading advertising agency in Los Angeles, said, "It's going to be about asking, 'What needs to happen in this particular situation, who are the five best people on the face of the earth to make that happen, and how do we bring them together to do it?'" (Barnette, 1993, p. 36).

John Stygles, a business development and research specialist in Natick, Massachusetts, worked for several virtual corporations that resembled the old "Mission Impossible" television show. "When they had an assignment, they pulled together their best people to handle it. When it was over, they all went back to their personal lives. So too with us. We pulled together to achieve a certain goal. When it was accomplished, we all went back to our regular lives. The structure of the virtual corporation is similar to that of a 'regular' corporation while the assignment is on. Loyalty to the goal or objective is what binds us together, not necessarily loyalty to a company" (Barnette, 1993).

Phillip Dyer, a project management professional in Atlanta, Georgia, founded Dyer Associates in 1990 as one employee outfit modeled along the lines of a virtual corporation. "The 'associates' part was to be a loosely connected network of pros who could offer more depth and breadth to clients than any one person. Maybe that's just old-fashioned networking, but now it's becoming recognized as a more 'legitimate' way of doing business" (Barnette, 1993).

The major issue in a virtual corporation is trust. People are often in a hurry to start with responsibilities and ownership issues. In order to make the relationships work in a virtual corporation, trust must be established first and foremost.

One of the concerns of VC members, since they do not work under one roof, rarely are in each others' presence except when an objective is being met, and lead regular lives away from the corporation, is who owns the property rights to information generated by the group? This again involves trust, and until there is agreement on who, what, and how, problems can arise among the participants in the virtual corporation.

The VC concept is new and exciting. Since there is no truly formal organizational structure, the question of who supervises whom arises. Certainly, in such a loosely knit gathering of experts, this issue needs addressed. Even after trust is established, there will need to be some semblance of leadership. Given the previous discussion in this paper regarding the nature of supervision, the virtual corporation's supervision must assume a Y-Theory management protocol. Each partner in the enterprise working on achieving the immediate objective for which the virtual corporation was formed needs to accept that the others in the corporation are working diligently on their particular part of the project. Without this trust, without this acceptance of the Y-Theory, the virtual corporation is doomed to failure.

Computer information is becoming more powerful as new technology is being developed. People are relying more and more on this type of information. In the pre-computer days, an employee would have to use their creativity, imagination, education, etc. to solve a problem. Now, it seems
that computers are taking away much of that innovative thinking.

Davidow and Malone (1991), in their seminal text, The Virtual Corporation, suggested that it is a meshing of the two (computer factor and human factor) that will make the VC successful.

Will employees become lazy in their thinking and not be as creative and innovative knowing or believing that information gathered through computers will solve their organizational decisions and problems? I think not. In fact, computers will only enhance the speed and productivity at which employees can complete the mundane tasks related to their jobs. Even in the treatment setting, computers now are being used to assess client's needs, write comprehensive and monthly treatment plans, quarterly progress reports, aftercare plans, maintain sophisticated client information in databases, wed human resources and training information to compile a complete employee work record, and communicate via e-mail.

There is no limit to the applications of computers in the VC and when the next round of CPU's get cheap and voice recognition gets more popular, the next quantum leap (no relation to the TV show) in human and computer interaction will take place. Keyboards limit the number of people willing to get a computer and manipulate the information for themselves. In our agency, those who can type are not afraid of interacting with the new technology. Those who cannot use the keyboard may find that voice recognition will certainly make users out of avoiders.

Imagine this for a moment. The counselor enters the office and says, "good morning Casper, what do we need to accomplish today?" The computer (Casper) responds, "the progress report on Fred Jones is due, and you have a treatment planning meeting at 10 am. You also need to finish the aftercare plan for Keith Hyatt. It's also your wife's birthday on Friday so get her a present." "Good", the human said. "give me the latest assessment summaries from the network." The computer then begins a narrated version of the assessment summaries. After listening to the summaries for a few moments, the human says, "print a copy of this summary for me." The computer says, "printing."

Is there some fear that computers will replace humans? I believe quite the reverse is true. Computers work for humans, not the other way around. As computers do more and more of the hack work, we get freed up to do the innovative work. Look at the businessman who gets to understand spreadsheets and the use of accounting software. Suddenly he can explore the parameters of his business during the time he used to spend just adding up the numbers. The problem is we are not moving up the level of human education and development at the same pace as we are gearing up the performance and capabilities of computers. The VC is predicated upon the new technology and the computer is at the hub of this communication network. It's not that humans will be less creative as a whole; it's that a divide is opening up between the advanced 'know how workers' (who will thrive in this future world) and the people who traditionally have relied on blue collar jobs (of which there will be less and less, and where there will be greater and greater volatility). We need to put the effort now into human education and development that we used to put into fighting wars and building factories.

And let's not sneer at being lazy. Laziness has been responsible for more good inventions than anything I know. Of course, not the kind of laziness that involves stupor but lying in bed creating things is not so lazy. Many extremely creative people get the most work done while lazily meditating. Napoleon and Einstein were two such individuals.

Time and space are two parameters that are being shrunk significantly in the Information Age. Davidow & Malone (1991) explored the value of time and how important it is when meeting a customer's need. They discussed how the VC concept made Wal-Mart such a successful company and maintained that Walton operated in a virtual setting. He put together his team of people focusing them on the areas in which they had expertise. He felt that they would be successful and make him successful in the areas that they knew well. His number one priority was meeting his customer's needs with enough inventory to satisfy customers but not be overstocked. He had a real thing about timing - when to open a new store and where. He felt the timing and place was extremely important for the success of that store. Today, Wal-Mart is the leader in discount stores.

In the years to come, incremental differences in an organization's ability to acquire, distribute, store, analyze, and invoke actions based on information will determine the winners and losers in the battle for customers regardless of what that organization is marketing, products or human services.

The authors stated, "the success of a virtual corporation will depend on its ability to gather and integrate a massive flow of information throughout its organizational components and intelligently act upon that information" (p. 123).

Information is the most valuable resource of the VC - even more than in a traditional corporation because it's really the only glue that binds the organization together. The old information flow mechanisms (eg. conversations at the water cooler, over the cubicle wall, formal meetings, informal hallway rendezvous, the tone of voice, the facial expression...) will no longer apply, so a fragment of information (possibly THE pivotal fragment) could easily fall through the cracks if it's not captured, analyzed, stored and distributed optimally. We carry a tremendous amount of information about people we know personally - not just appearance, but what they know, so we know who to go to for an answer. What is the VC equivalent? It's only the fragile web of what we can glean from messages and resumes.

The real key is to weave the change into the fabric of the preexisting organization. That's where VC's enter the picture IF the participants have the HUMAN skills of rapidly creating and recreating temporary organizations.

The ultimate goal of the VC is to create quality while limiting cost. Philip Crosby (1991), an early observer of VC, "estimated that the cost of poor quality could be as great as 20% and that, with processes that eliminate defects and wastes, most of that money could be saved." Crosby came up with four commandments of product quality:

1. **Definition** - Quality is the performance to requirements
2. **System** - The prevention of defects
3. **Performance standard** - Zero defects
4. **Measurements** - The price of nonconformance to perfect quality"

The following **TEN commandments of Quality Improvement** govern the VC:

1. Never stop improving. There is no such thing as perfect quality.
2. Quality is everybody's business, from janitor to board chair.
3. Keep your eyes, ears and nose open ... the best quality ideas are only as good as the ability of your senses to detect them.
4. Develop a detailed implementation plan. Talking about quality is not quality.
5. Foster cooperation ... turf is the worst enemy of quality.
6. Dissect every job. Discarding the unnecessary is as relevant to quality as is measuring the necessary.

7. Control ALL processes, not only production processes. The organization must know all the factors that impact quality lest it repair the wrong ones when things go badly.
8. Make extraordinary efforts when things go wrong. Your attitude and level of effort during difficult times are the ultimate measures of quality.
9. Think beyond improving profits. The benefits of quality are too important to be reduced to mere fiscal measures.
10. Be patient. Do not look for the benefits of this quarter's quality improvements only in the next quarter (Davidow & Malone, 1991).

I believe EVERYONE in a company is responsible for quality. Not just quality of the product, but quality of customer support, etc. Nothing frustrates me more than to be enjoying a new product (such as software) but need some additional information and get jerked around by the customer support people. On the flip side, nothing turns me off as a buyer faster than to call a marketing department to get additional information on something and getting jerked around there. I forget the product no matter how good it sounds. I'm also what Faith Popcorn has called an "attack consumer". If I get jerked around too bad, I start chewing my way up the chain of command until I'm satisfied.

So most corporate quality programs (there are shining exceptions) are doomed from the beginning by a power hierarchy which cannot face its own quality nakedness. It is easier for an entrenched corporate management to allow an IBM to fail, than it is for them to admit their own culpability on the way to a recovery. This is not only an issue of quality, but may possibly be a law of nature, like entropy, which can be called the **Law of Evolutionary Thickets**. This means that the more an organization (or an organism) evolves by way of specialization, the more it becomes hemmed in by constraints which hamper both its ability to function AND its ability to change. The cheetah is a rather beautiful and tragic example of this happening in nature.

However, in organizational life there is no excuse since organizations are human endeavors and people are endowed with the analytical and cognitive skills which obligate them as managers to manage and escape from, rather than drift into and succumb to the thicket of impenetrable lethargy.

TQM applied to the virtual corporation is listening to the customer and implementing the desires of the customer into the design, manufacture and distribution of the product or service. What makes it "virtual" is the way technology is used to collect and analyze the voice of the consumers.

Davidow & Malone (1991) discussed the future relationship between producers and customers and how it will affect the virtual concept. Here are some highlighted points:

1. The nature of new business relationships will result in stronger and more enduring ties based on mutual destiny shared by both suppliers and customers.
2. The VC may appear amorphous and in perpetual flux but will be nestled within a tight network of relationships.
3. Common future and mutual support will be highlights of the relationship between producers and customers
4. Customers will depend on producers having more invested in the relationship - they will share business secrets, train them to their needs, integrate them into their design process (p. 152).

The question now is will this change of relationship happening now occur quickly enough for the organizations to more freely accept the concept of the VC and virtual teams?

I believe Davidow & Malone are being very idealistic in their predictions. I hope they are right. The American business paradigm has been based on competition; the above characteristics assume a more cooperative model. That's a major shift in thinking for our economic environment (competition for capital) and our culture. I believe the competitive model business in which we currently operate deters the formation of the VC, especially when dealing with individuals because our society tends to value the individual and measures him/her competitively in relation to his/her peers. We learn that model from our very first days in school. The problems associated with forming VCs, reflect difficulties over managing individuals and their unique needs for money, security, recognition, power, and self-actualization.

Can services be seen as virtual items? Does it get confusing when we begin talking about a virtual service? Products are easy to define because they are tangible. Services are not so. It seems that the service industry, like the alcohol and drug treatment field that I am in, may have a more difficult time adapting to the virtual concept and idea than the product industry.

As the shift from the industrial age to the information age takes place, there will be a shift in the way capital and labor interact. In the Post Capitalist Society, Drucker (1993) posits that we are making a transition from a capitalist economy, where capital and labor are the commodities of trade, to an economy where the application of knowledge and ideas are paramount. Alvin Toffler (1992) makes a similar prediction in his book "Powershift."

There is no question that rules governing supervisor/employee relationships are shifting rapidly in the face of human capital, which has spawned a new term... the "preferred employer." More and more we have to manage people as if they're volunteers...another Drucker idea.

Davidow & Malone (1991) stated, "in the virtual corporation, where almost every employee is to one degree or another a leader, the requirements for belief and trust are greater than ever before" (p. 183).

The authors further suggested that not only does the relationship of line staff and middle management's' roles change with the organization in a VC, but also the CEO. They stated the following characteristics that a CEO in a VC should have:
1.   "The CEO must define the corporate vision and skillfully convey it to all employees at every level"

2. "The CEO must symbolize the company"
3. "The CEO must be the company's premier generalist"
4. "The CEO must trust the employees of his firm"

It appears that CEO's will have to change a lot in their management style. The CEO will need to become more involved in every aspect of their company, as well as, more involved with their employees.

As organizations change their way of doing business to the virtual corporation concept, what happens to business management courses? Will a whole new curriculum have to be developed to include this new way of thinking and doing business? Davidow & Malone stated, "middle management's function has been to serve as an information channel through which top managers can view events and to relay orders down to the individuals doing the work. These functions have become unnecessary because computer networks can carry much of the information about the status of operations more efficiently and effectively than can people" (p. 183).

Eventually, I believe the whole concept of layered management, i.e. upper, middle, and then the "peons" will disappear. In many ways it's a featherbedding-based system used to award cronies and good ol' boys rather than competence. Business will get more like sports, where the individual either contributes to the team or he or she does not wear the uniform.

Information conduit is only one of the roles that a supervisor plays. If one accepts the notion that the majority of people perform to less than their capacity, then it makes sense that another role of a supervisor is to facilitate high-performance on the part of the subordinates. Motivating individual employees will become the primary responsibility of supervisors.

Middle management has made itself an endangered species because it has not adequately played the coach role. It has failed to obtain high performance from those it supervises? One of the major criticisms of middle managers under the traditional organizational structure is that they "manage upward" and spend most of their energies being corporate politicians rather than carrying out their duty to develop those they supervise. This is a major waste of creative energy and needs to change if there is hope for the present industrial-style managed organizations to successfully evolve into an information-age system.

There will always be "human factor" problems. At the working level, supervisors and "lower" managers deal with people directly in groups of 7-20 or so depending on the complexities of the work place be it physical or virtual. These team leaders facilitate brainstorming and coordinate the immediate problems of the work space like scheduling, resolving conflicts of personality, and performance issues. But there are problems between work groups that need resolution and the task of generating information still requires humans.

Granted, the computer can relay directives and report meeting results between senior management and work groups and workers and computers can do some pretty remarkable things with raw (reliable) data, but there is still the question of determining what data should be collected, which process to apply to distill it to an informative level, and how to insure its validity. These tasks can be delegated to "middle managers."

These challenges lend themselves to "ad-hoc" assignments of "specialists" or "expediters" who apply the human touch to those situations that need them and solve the one-time problems like how to distill collected data into usable information. These "staff" functions required lots of people in the absence of mechanical information processors, but some of the tasks will never be replaced (automated).

In the near future, organizations will become more effective by moving toward small groups of autonomous workers. Large companies are fragmenting and there is less and less need for large sets of workers doing similar jobs. The function of middle managers primarily carrying through the initiatives and policies laid down by senior executives is certainly doomed. What is needed now is initiative and policy making 'on the hoof' by ALL managers - indeed in many companies, by all employees. Read Tom Peters on 'empowerment'. If middle managers do not behave like executives - make important decisions all the time - their role will eventually become obsolete.

Management and supervision will change in the virtual corporation concept. "The most fundamental transition will be the shift that management will have to make from directing action to ensuring the smooth functioning of processes. A second change will occur in the very structure of management itself. It will become less hierarchical and in the process much of middle management will vanish" (Davidow & Malone, 1991, p. 194).

I agree with this statement. There will be a difference in management today vs. management in the virtual concept. The mind set of managers will change. Supervisors will need to be very flexible. They will need to expand their thinking, do more brainstorming, and basically become more communicative.

Nagler & Hibino (1992) suggested some unique approaches to solving problems, and generating ideas that may provide those organizations contemplating the transition to a VC to consider. The main points described by the authors are:

The Purposes Principle: Focusing on purposes helps strip away nonessential aspects to avoid working on the wrong problem.

The Solution-After-Next Principle: Innovation can be stimulated and solutions made more effective by working backward from an ideal solution.

The Systems Principle: Every problem is part of a larger system. Understanding the elements and dimensions of a system matrix lets you determine in advance the complexities you must incorporate in the implementation of the solution.

The Limited Information Principle: Knowing too much about a problem initially can prevent you from seeing some excellent alternative solutions.

The People Design Principle: The people who will carry out and use a solution must work together in developing the solution with Breakthrough Thinking. The proposed solution should include only the minimal, critical details, so that the users of the solution can have some flexibility in applying it.

The Betterment Timeline Principle: A sequence of purpose-directed solutions is a bridge to a better future. A philosophy professors once asked his students to think about the differences in efficiency between Democracy and Totalitarianism or Dictatorship. His point was that our society's way of conducting government business is woefully inefficient compared to the ability of other systems to decide and take action.

Yet over the long run, it is our society that has produced better results for itself both in terms of standard of living and educated people. Why is it that in spite of our inefficiencies, or because of them, we have been successful?

Our planned inefficiencies give us an opportunity to think, to hear and explore alternatives, to be open to ideas that are quantum levels better than our old ways.

I believe the same is true with organizations. The old-style hierarchical structure parallels totalitarianism. Frankly, it can be awesomely efficient. Eventually, it stifles creativity and lateral thinking (deBono, 1970). But the new-style structure is a matrix. Supervisors cannot rely on automatic obedience to implement their will, but must influence and discuss and be open to compromise and new ideas. As with a free and open society, I believe that the price of a little inefficiency will be more than compensated by the great things that can be achieved by free and empowered work force.

The main benefit of democracy is that it allows rich variety and the opportunity to make plenty of 'mistakes' (that's how we learn) and plenty of novelty (that's how we progress). The rigid organization (nationally or in a company) stifles initiative and assumes that the "central office" is right. But in a world of chaos, how can it be right more than (at best) 50% of the time?

I believe the most difficult issue for senior managers and supervisors will be learning to influence without having to control. Most people think that this is impossible to do. A great deal of time will be spent with trainers, facilitators, and counselors helping supervisors with this issue.

The biggest issue for senior supervisors will be in making some key shifts:
1. From management to leadership;
2. From delegating to empowering;
3. From criticizing to coaching;
4. From making excuses to being accountable.

In order for the VC to work, everyone in the virtual corporation must clearly understand, on a very personal level, what the vision of the organization is. All the goal setting and objective discussion in the world does not substitute for people really internalizing the organization's vision.

When people get it - there is magic. When they don't, there is confusion at best and destruction at worst.

Some companies that have or are using work teams as internal VC components have produced some interesting results. Here are a few examples:

1.   So successful have teamwork programs been at the Defense System and Electronics Group at Texas Instruments that management announced the goal of having every employee in a self-directed work team by the end of 1992.

2.   A Federal Express work team identified a billing problem that was costing the company $2.1 million per year.

3.   Aetna Life & Casualty reduced the ratio of middle managers at its home office from 1:7 to 1:20 while still improving customer service.

4.   Work teams at Johnsonville Foods in Wisconsin convinced their CEO to make a major plant expansion, and the result has been a 50% improvement in productivity."

Johnston and Packer (1987) suggested that the baby boomers group will be the last group in our lifetime that will include the stereotype of the average American worker which is, "white and male". They stated, "among the twenty-five million new workers in this decade, only 15% will fit this profile. Forty two percent will be women, a group that historically has not migrated to technical careers; 20% will be native (nonimmigrant American) nonwhite men and women; and 22% will immigrants, many of whom will have to learn English" (p. 123).

As a marketing tactic, it is the ultimate "have it your way" campaign. In our business we have won new customers by responding to their needs. When the issue of how to treat "drug sellers" arose, our agency created a special "drug sellers" program that employed a relatively unknown concept called Criminal Personality Theory pioneered by Yochelson and Samenow (1970). Responding to a probation request for an innovative program to treat juvenile delinquents who were not drug sellers or chemically abusive or dependent, a Youth Leadership Program was researched and approved for inception. Combining the best of the military, boot camp model, education, and the Outward Bound Wilderness Experience, this program will serve a growing niche of delinquents in the juvenile justice system.

Strategic marketing will not be part of the virtual corporation. In its place will become, "marketing of value". More emphasis will be placed on the relationship to the customer - basically - keeping them happy. Davidow and Malone (1991) suggested that reliability, creditability and trust are key factors in customer relationships. They stated, "the task of the virtual corporation is to develop relationships with customers to enable them to obtain the maximum value from the product they have purchased" (p. 189).

In order to evolve into a VC, organizations will need to transform their already established management and supervision practices into a continuing support system. The management of these companies will need to change their way of thinking, managing, and training their leadership. Change will not happen overnight, but I believe, if organizations are serious about developing into a virtual corporation, they will need to start now to change. The information age arrived five years ago in 1987.

12. SUPERVISION IN THE 21ST CENTURY

Supervision in the 21st Century is destined to change. In the Information Age, the organizations that will survive will be those which emulate the VC. Products and services will be customized by organizations who realize that the "customer" is boss.

The role of the educational establishment will be critical in ensuring that it produces the kinds of leaders and employees which will readily adapt to this new type of system and its philosophy, thinking, and approaches to managing information and human resources effectively and efficiently. It is necessary that supervisors in all organizations realize the paramount importance of training for adults in business and industrial settings. Concurrently, supervisors in education need to revamp the primary, secondary, and post-secondary learning environments to adequately prepare those who are about to enter the national and international work forces so they will be ready to undertake the challenges which lie ahead.

Educational supervision was not the primary focus of this paper. In fact, no specific type of organizational supervision was diagnosed and evaluated. My goal was to provide an overview of the entire range of behaviors, attitudes, and beliefs related to supervision and its role.

The new millennium is rapidly approaching. Preparing for it will be no small task. The infrastructure of many of our industrial, educational, social service, and business organizations are collapsing. The information age is forcing new ideas and behaviors on people everywhere. Management without effective communication becomes mismanagement. Time and space are no longer static, but fluid and dynamic. Unless managers at all levels accept this reality and begin to work with it to improve those infrastructures, many organizations are doomed to receivership or Chapter 11 status.

In education, the same issues are present. Many superintendents, principals, and head teachers still do not accept the concept of the information age. Few schools are gearing up to meet the demands of the new social and world order. There is a preference among most educational personnel to maintain the status quo. When attendance drops, and students fail, administrators and teachers place blame on students, their families, the society, and many other external factors which are out of their control. They avoid accepting responsibility for creating new educational environments which will prepare the next generation for assimilation into the information age.

On NBC news recently, a segment was aired on a school in Rockford, Michigan which accepted this challenge. The entire school is organized to facilitate experiential learning and mastering the technology of the information age. Students use all the modern communication technology to learn. Even skills such as effective parenting are taught within the daily schedule. The school operates a day care center in which students and teachers watch children and learn how to effectively care for them. News reports and other daily communication activities are written, produced, and directed by students with faculty assistance. At 4 PM the students go home, but the school is not vacated. Each evening, adults utilize the same facilities to learn how to deal with the modern technology, and prepare for new jobs and careers in the information age. The 40 million dollar price tag for the school seems to be well spent. Unlike most schools which lie dormant for three months a year, the Rockford School never closes its doors.

This is just one example of the kind of innovative thinking which can prepare the learners of the next generation for the challenges of the future which is already upon us.

What kinds of changes in beliefs, attitudes, and behaviors on the part of leaders, politicians, supervisors, managers, will be necessary to affect these changes? How will they facilitate such changes so the gap between what is and what will be are decreased?

These are my notions regarding what needs to occur before this nation of diverse organizations, businesses, industries, social agencies, and educational establishments will be prepared for the inevitable information age future:

1. ***Stop denying the birth of the information age and begin to accept it.*** Until this denial that the world is evolving toward another era is embraced by the top leaders in our nation and our organizations, whether they be businesses, industries, education, or human services, we will continue to lag behind the times and be at the effect of the waves of changes crashing upon our shores.

2. ***Encourage the education of computer literacy*** **from kindergarten to the Ph.D. level and beyond.** It amazes me how many top managers, educators, social service, and business people still are not computer literate. As long as a secretary can type a memo, even if he or she uses a word processor, and the manager does not have to interact with the technology, this condition will continue to exist. Secretaries are no longer just typists, but information managers. The effective supervisor needs to understand and accept this new role. Countless hours of top management's time is wasted in interacting with a secretary who is still perceived as a "clerk-typist." Personal Data Assistants (PDA) are rapidly gaining acceptance and as the prices drop in the near future, the information management once delegated to a secretary will no longer be necessary.

3. ***Eliminate copy machines and begin to use electronic forms of communication*** **which are much cheaper, more efficient, and environmentally sound.** Books on CD's are much easier to produce and reproduce, lighter to carry around and distribute, and once CD copy technology is affordable, this method of exchanging information will certainly speed up the learning curve. E-mail, and FAX modems will add to the expeditious exchange of information between individuals, and among the leaders of diverse organizations. Cellular phones already dot the landscape. Driving in heavy freeway traffic this past week in metropolitan

Pittsburgh, I observed nearly every other driver near me animatedly talking on a car phone. As the cellular networks branch out and even rural areas are connected, the global village will be everywhere there is a phone, and not necessarily a line. Brainstorm software which permits many people to share threads of information over networks across time and space will eventually eliminate the need for people to meet face to face. Only the most important affairs will demand such meetings.

4. ***Begin to measure competencies rather than abstract learning potential.*** Many talented individuals are eliminated from successful personal careers because they do not possess math and reading skills which are only two of the 206 domains of learning currently measurable. The SAT scores are not the only measures of an individual's abilities. Many fine tradespeople would fail the SAT test, but easily can program a computer, fix an automobile, a refrigerator or some other modern appliance. We need to foster the rebuilding of the apprenticeship type training process to prepare for the vast amount of technical repair work which will arise from the explosion of all this high tech gear. Blue collar workers will evolve into blue lab coat workers.

5. ***Train administrators, supervisors, and employees in the concepts of the Virtual Corporation.*** As time and space expand, organizations will need to adapt to the changes facing them. Smaller, mobile, efficient work groups of experts will replace the monolithic structures we now see choking on their last gasps as the information age consumes their air. Organizational development concepts may need to be changed from OD to ORD, organizational redevelopment. Too many organizations today are top heavy with management and the middle managers within these organizations are incapable or unwilling to act without permission

from above. As deBono described, there is a need for lateral as well as vertical thinking. There is a critical need for lateral expansion of organizations away from the purely vertical structures which currently dominate our culture. Policies will need to be replaced. Fewer rewards for political activities and greater ones for creative endeavors need to be fostered. Meshing the human factor and the computer factor will enhance the merging of vertical and lateral organizational structures until an effective matrix is established as described by Davidow and Malone (1991).

6. ***Manage people with democratic rather than totalitarian principles.*** Since the X-Theory management style still predominates, there is an immediate need to reframe this management style and move immediately toward a universal acceptance of the Y-Theory, and eventually the Z-Theory of management. In the work environment, too many people experience little influence over a part of their lives which consumes fully a third of them. This is an intolerable condition for most individuals. The result is often low motivation, little loyalty to the organization, and turnover rates which cost dearly. As employees are empowered to take ownership of their direct work-related responsibilities, this condition will improve. However, it is supervision's role to not only foster but facilitate and support this change. Perhaps, that is what GM meant when it advertised Saturn as "not just another car company." Blue-chip GM went outside its organizational structure to create a creative, dynamic foster child which seems to be unique in the car manufacturing world. (I just wish they would produce a cheaper version of their automobile like VW did back in the early 1960's).

7.   ***Reward creative, productive enterprise.*** For too long, rewards in most organizations were based upon politics rather than achieving results. This trend needs to be reversed if the organizations presently existing hope to survive in the future. Politics as usual is destroying the nation-state and many of the organizations which exist within it today. As long as they still maintain nepotistic, "good ol' boy" networks and internally choke off the life blood of their systems, they are doomed to failure. Vertical thinking is encouraged, but lateral thinking avoided. Only in the most progressive organizations do "think tanks" exist. The need for all types of thinking patterns to be fostered within organizational structures cannot be overemphasized. Brainstorming is not enough. An organizational culture must be established in which all ideas are considered. **PO** (deBono, 1972) must replace the Yes/No mentality which governs today.

7.   ***Realize that Time and Space are diminishing.*** There is time to wait, but only if the time is not important. The global village is rapidly approaching. From my home in the most rural part of Pennsylvania, with my computer and phone line, I am connected with the world. Five years ago, the connection cost was prohibitive. In just one year, the modem which I purchased for $100 (2400 Baud) is outdated. For a few dollars more, I can now own a 14,400 Baud FAX modem which is six times faster and performs more functions at less cost. Organizations which avoid the use of this technology are doomed. In organizations where the technology is embraced but supervisors refuse to use it, they will slowly destroy their organizations from within. Hard copy memos, which cost from $5-20 to produce and distribute to all employees need to be replaced by e-mail messages which can be sent for micro-pennies.

8. ***Foster lifelong learning at all levels of the organization,*** **beginning with supervision.** We must accept that what worked today probably will not work tomorrow. This is a most painful lesson. Not many supervisors are prepared to entertain a program of life long learning. Yet without such activity on the part of supervisors in business, industry, education, and human services, the future for these individuals is murky. There is too much to learn about the future to be caught unaware. Management training is not enough. Each individual supervisor must accept responsibility for undertaking a personal program of lifelong learning to enhance his or her growth and development.

9. ***Learn how to learn.*** Learning how to learn is the key. Memorizing information is not necessary. Let the PDA keep track of phone numbers, memos, and other data. Access information needed with the touch of a pen. Learn how to use the technology to do a much better, more efficient, and less costly job. With the information explosion, it is impossible to learn everything about even the most microscopic facets of any one subject. What is most important is learning how to learn, how to think, and how to solve problems practically, swiftly, and efficiently. One of my favorite quotes is "You don't have a problem if you have a solution." If the problem is getting information, the solution is using the technology to speed up the search process. Knowing where to find something is more important than being able to memorize what the information is. Computers permit this process to happen expeditiously. All sorts of databases exist which make this a reality and not just a "what if." Dialogue, Compuserve, IQuest, NASA, ERIC, Psychlit, and numerous corporate and private BBS's are readily available to individuals who are willing to use them to enhance their learning.

10. ***Find an acceptable, personal balance of body, mind, and spirit.*** In times which are turbulent such as this transitional generation from the industrial to the information age, balancing body, mind, and spirit becomes a necessity and not a luxury. Demands upon supervisors, employees, all people are sometimes extreme. Problems abound. Decisions are made at a whirlwind pace. Processing the necessary information to conduct even the minimal amount of business is perplexing. It is at these times that the supervisor who finds the necessary balance in his or her work, personal, and spiritual life will succeed. The problems a supervisor faces can often be ameliorated by finding this balance. What is exciting about this endeavor is that the end product produces for the supervisor a measure of equanimity in his or her life that makes the work life more productive and the personal life far more exciting.

Supervision is the 21st Century will be exciting, challenging, and fulfilling. As time and space shrink, possibilities will expand. The shrewd supervisor will expand with them. He or she will begin to see the "What If's" as diamonds in the rough. No longer will the quantum leap in communication technology frighten him or her. Instead, it will prompt new thinking, new awareness, new creations which will make organizations roar with power, turbocharged by an overwhelming desire to expand beyond Yes/No and escape the "land of pretend" and enter the family of man living in a global village connected by invisible threads of fiber optics and laser beams from satellites floating silently hundreds of miles above the planet, Earth.

Forward!

REFERENCES

A.A. International. (1954). The big book. New York: A.A.
Press.

Alberti, R.E., & Emmons, M.L. (1975). Stand up, speak out,
talkback. New York: Pocket Books.

Bach, G.R., & Goldberg, H. (1974). Creative aggression. New
York: Harper & Row.

Barnette, M. (1993). The ethereal company: virtual corporations.
Compuserve Magazine, 12,11, 38-39.

Bower, S.A., & Bower, G. (1976). Asserting yourself. Reading,
Mass.: Addison-Wesley.

Butler, P. (1976). Self-assertion for women: A guide to becoming
androgynous. New York: Harper & Row.

Cotler, S.B., & Guerra, J.J. (1976). Assertiveness training: A
humanistic-behavioral guide to self-dignity. Champaign, Ill:
Research Press.

Davidow, W.H., & Malone, M.S. (1991). The virtual corporation.
New York: Harper & Row.

deBono, E. (1991). Six action shoes. New York: Harper Collins
Publishers.

deBono, E. (1985). Six thinking hats. Boston: Little, Brown, and
Company.

deBono, E. (1972). PO: beyond yes and no. London: Penguin
Books.

deBono, E. (1970). Lateral thinking. London: Penguin Books.

deBono, E. (1976). Teaching thinking. London: Penguin Books.

deBono, E. (1971). Practical thinking. London: Penguin Books.

deBono, E. (1985). deBono's thinking course. New York: Fact On
File Publications.

Drucker, P.S. (1993). Post capitalist society. New York: Harper
Business.

Drury, S. (1981). Assertive supervision: Successful management of
people. Unpublished training manual. (Available from (1613
Orchard Lane, Arden, Delaware 19810).

Drury, S.S. (1984). Assertive supervision. Champaign, Illinois:
Research Press.

Eisen, J. (1984). Power talk. New York: Simon & Schuster.

George, C.S. (1970). Management for business and industry.
Englewood Cliffs, New Jersey: Prentice-Hall, Inc.

George, C.S. (1979). Supervision in action: The art of managing others. Reston, Virginia: Prentice-Hall.

Haney, W.B. (1986). Communication and interpersonal relations: Text and cases. Homewood, Illinois: Irwin.

Harrison, F.C. (1989). Spirit of leadership. Germantown, Tenn: Leadership Education and Development Corp.

Henley, N.M. (1977). Body politics: Power, sex and nonverbal,communication. Englewood   Cliffs, N.J.: Prentice-Hall.

Jakubowski, P., & Lange, A.J. (1978). The assertive options: Your rights and responsibilities. Champaign, Ill.: Research Press.

Johnston, J., & Packer, K. (1987). Workforce 2000: Work and workers for the 21st century. New York: Hudson Institute for the Department of Labor.

Keirsey, D. & Bates, M. (1984). Please understand me: Character & temperament types. Del Mar, California: Gnosology Books.

Kerzner, H. (1982). Project management for executives. New York: Van Nostrand Reinhold.

Korda, M. (1975). Power. New York: Random House.

McGregor, D. (1957). Adventures in thought and action: Proceedings of the Fifth Anniversary   Convocation of the School of Industrial Management, Massachusetts Institute of Technology, Cambridge, April 9, 1957, p. 28.

McGregor, D. (1960). The human side of enterprise. New York: McGraw-Hill.

Maslow, A.H. (1954). Motivation and personality. New York: Harper & Row.

Nadler, G., & Hibino, S. (1992). Breaking thinking. Los Angeles: Prima Publishing & Communications.

Peters, T.J., & Waterman, R.H. (1982). In search of excellence Lessons from the best run companies. New York: Harper & Row.

Ringer, R. (1977). Looking out for #1. Beverly Hills, Calif.: The Los Angeles Book Corporation.

Robbins, A. (1885). Personal power. Los Angeles: Robbins Institute International.

Smith, M. (1975). When I say no I feel guilty. New York: Dial Press.

www.ingramcontent.com/pod-product-compliance
Lightning Source LLC
Chambersburg PA
CBHW070811180526
45168CB00002B/573